D1444827

CHRISTIAN–MUSLIM RELATIONS

Christian–Muslim Relations

A Case Study of Sarawak, East Malaysia

THEODORE GABRIEL

Avebury

Aldershot • Brookfield USA • Singapore • Sydney

LUTHER SEMINARY
LIBRARY
2375 Como Avenue
St. Paul, MN 55108-1447

BP172
.G24

© Theodore Gabriel 1996

All rights reserved. No part of this publication may be reproduced, stored in a retrieval system, or transmitted in any form or by any means, electronic, mechanical, photocopying, recording or otherwise without the prior permission of the publisher.

Published by
Avebury
Ashgate Publishing Limited
Gower House
Croft Road
Aldershot
Hants GU11 3HR
England

Ashgate Publishing Company
Old Post Road
Brookfield
Vermont 05036
USA

A CIP catalogue record for this book is available from the British Library

ISBN 1 85972 325 X

Library of Congress Catalog Card Number: 96-85202

Printed and bound by Athenaeum Press, Ltd., Gateshead, Tyne & Wear.

LUTHER LIBRARY
2375 Como Avenue
St. Paul, MN 55108-1447

tla 00 - 20084

Contents

List of tables and maps

Foreword

Dr. Gabriel's fine study of Christian-Muslim relations in the Malay state of Sarawak should be of interest to all concerned both with international relations and with inter-faith dialogue, for inter-faith dialogue all too frequently gives the impression, particularly to those of us who work in the field of the study of religions, of moving in an ideational realm far removed from the actualities of interfaith relationships on the ground. I can think of no better way for those engaged in such dialogue of being brought down to earth than by reading and re-reading Dr. Gabriel's meticulously researched and extremely judicious book.

With much graphic illustration, and by references to both Government policy and to the mind-sets of both Chrstians and Muslims in Sarawak, Dr. Gabriel shows the difficulties and the possibilities of establishing a tolerant working relationship between people of differing faiths in an area of the world where Islam has recently become a major political and social force. As such it can be said to provide a test case for Islam's ability when in power in an area with long established alternative religious traditions to provide the political and social framework for communities of differing religious faith and cultures to live together in harmony. For Dr. Gabriel's judgement of the successes and failures of this experiment so far, the reader must of course read the book, but if religious policy in the predominantly Muslim country of Malaysia is the test case that I believe it to be for Islam, then the book should be of interest not just to the readership that I have indicated, but to all those seeking to understand the role of Islam in the world today and, perhaps more importantly, in the world tomorrow -- and that means, or should mean, all of us.

James Thrower
Professor of the History of Religions in the University of Aberdeen.

Preface

In the summer of 1993 I spent a fascinating fortnight in Sarawak, mainly in the beautiful city of Kuching. This was part of a project which aimed to study Christian-Muslim relations in this the biggest of all Malaysian states. I chose Sarawak for my study because of its distinctive demographic characteristics vis-a-vis peninsular Malaysia. Moreover, it is a fact that the Malaysian states of Borneo have been much less the subject of scholarly study than the other parts of the Federation. This is no doubt being set right now, but even then the number of published scholarly sources for the study of Sarawak is limited in comparison with those available for Peninsular Malaysia. I have therefore had to rely to a large extent on my own researches in Sarawak, on personal interviews and on other primary sources such as the *Sarawak Gazette*. However, several of the issues which I discuss in this, for instance, Islamic resurgence, are of general relevance to Malaysia as a whole and standard works on Malaysia such as the volumes by Negata and Gordon P Means, and other book, have been very helpful in the preparation of this book. But Sarawak has a distinctiveness of its own, which I have stressed in my discussions, and which I hope comes out clearly in this book.

Being an Indian I have drawn on my Indian experience to throw light on some of the issues such as pluralism and consequent problems in inter-religious/ethnic relations that India and Malaysia share. Both are nations which have fairly recently thrown off the colonial yoke and are adjusting to the new democratic way of life and government. It is inevitable that in such a situation the political configurations are in a state of flux and will take time to crystallise and settle into a state of greater stability. But it is salutary that both nations have in comparison to other fledgling states freed from former autocratic regimes, succeeded in persisting with the democratic form of government in spite of many problems, and have not lapsed into military rule, dictatorship or other forms of undemocratic regimes. Both are vibrant nations, emerging from the long slumber of colonial rule and are working hard to find their own identity and place in the comity of nations. I have no doubt that both have lessons to learn from each other's experience. The comparisons I have made occasionally are, I hope, therefore relevant and useful. The observations I have occasionally made about the Hindu community of India relate mainly to extremist organisations and political parties, and should not be construed as pejorative of the community as a whole or of this great religion as such. The vast majority of Hindus have proved themselves in the past as now to be tolerant, peaceful and following an ideology based on ahimsa, non-violence.

I have been a student and teacher of Islamic Studies for a number of years now, and I have the greatest respect and admiration for the faith of Islam and its adherents. I follow the Christian faith myself, but that has in no way prevented me from taking an unbiassed view of the issues arising from the interaction of these two great religions in Malaysia. Throughout my research and the writing of this short monograph my sole objective has been to get at the truth. The fact that I am not a Malaysian myself has perhaps helped me to maintain this objectivity. I will be very happy if this book has been able to offer some constructive suggestions for the improvement of inter-ethnic and inter-religious relations in Sarawak.

My interest in Malaysia was initially sparked when I made a number of good friends among my former Malaysian colleagues in the University of Aberdeen, who were pursuing their doctoral studies in the Department of Religious Studies there, and with many of whom I still keep in touch. I know that one of them Dr.Ghazzali Basri has ben working on a volume on Christian-Muslim Relations in Malaysia. I hope this monograph would be a useful supplement to Dr Basri's work. An immediate link with Sarawak has been my former student, Rev. Dennis Gimang, who was my host in Sarawak and who helped me immeasurably in the course of my researches there. I also acknowledge with thanks and great appreciation the personages who granted me interviews. I also wish to express my gratitude to the authorities of the College of Higher Education in Cheltenham for the grant awarded to me for this project which made my visit to Sarawak possible. Special mention must be made of Ms. Kathryn Sharp, cartographer to the College Department of Geography, whose skill and professionalism is reflected in the accurate and neat maps included in this monograph. I am very grateful to my former teacher, and a reputed scholar of religion, Professor James Thrower of the University of Aberdeen for such an excellent foreword to the book, highlighting the significance of the issues currently under debate in Malaysia. I finally wish to acknowledge the immense help given by my daughter Sunayana who patiently typed up my manuscript from my almost illegible writing, and Mrs. Lyn Godwin and Mrs. Patricia Downes who helped me to prepare the camera ready copy of my manuscript.

Theodore Gabriel

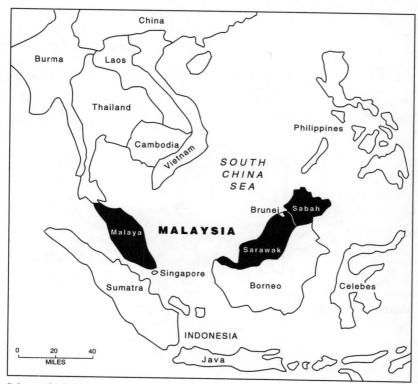

Map of Malaysia

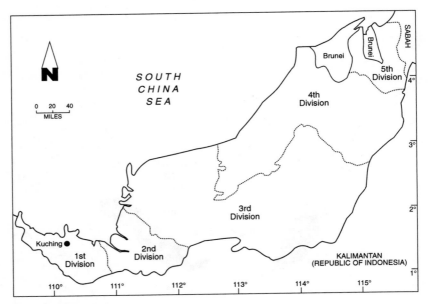

Map of Sarawak

1 Introduction

Sarawak is part of Borneo, the third largest island in the world, and together with Sabah is that part of the Federation of Malaysia known as East Malaysia.

Malaysia has one the most diverse populations in the world, with many ethnic, religious and linguistic divisions. India, one of her large neighbours, is also demographically quite diverse. But unlike Malaysia, India is vastly Caucasoid Indo-Aryan and Dravidian and the Hindu religious community forms about 80% of the population. In Malaysia on the other hand, the Malay/ Muslim ethno-religious group is only just over 50% of the population and there are substantial numbers of Chinese and Indians in the federation, resulting in a more evenly balanced demographic mixture. However it is interesting to note that the Malaysian constitution incorporates what can be viewed as rather discriminatory provisions advantageous to the Malays, such as reservations in employment, not only in the public, but also in the private sector, promotions to higher positions, admission to educational institutions, allotment of public funds for projects, grant of commercial and other licenses et al. These are purportedly for the advancement of the Malays, who are seen as a backward community economically and educationally, but not socially, as compared to the Chinese and Indian communities. The Indian constitution also has similar concessions and privileges for deprived sections of society, the scheduled castes and tribes, but then these groups form a much smaller proportion of the population than the so-called forward communities -- upper caste Hindus, Christians etc. The Malaysian provision is extraordinary in that the "positive discrimination" is aimed at the numerically dominant group, the Malay Muslims. The normal practice logically would be for a majority and politically powerful group to support weaker and numerically less populous sections of society. In Malaysia the reverse seems to be the case and thus these provisions should inevitably lead to imbalances in the political, economical and social spheres. In Malaysia the constitutional provisions of perks for Malays are designed to bring them up to the economic and educational standards of the Chinese and Indian sections of the nation. However, there are many critics who opine that these privileges have benefitted only the higher echelons of Malay society, especially those in urban areas, and have not been able to uplift the rural fishermen / peasant sections of the Malaysian community.(1) Even if the N.E.P. (National Economic Policy) had been advantageous to the Malay community, a majority being supported by resources essentially from a minority would only serve in the long term to generate imbalances in the opposite direction. Fortunately in Malaysia the numerical disparities between the majority and the minority is minimal, unlike in the Indian case, thus the imbalances would become palpable only in the distant future. Even in India after about five decades of constitutional concessions for the scheduled castes and tribes, dissatisfaction has been simmering in the forward communities such as the higher Hindu castes about what they see as the essential injustice and discriminatory ideology of the constitutional provisions. This recently led to the overthrow of the V.P. Singh government in Delhi when they tried to increase the quota of reservations for the scheduled groups in Government employment. (There the reservations apply only to the public sector) In India the concessions to the Harijans etc. have to be considered by parliament and renewed every ten years, whereas in Malaysia the privileges accorded to the

Malay/Bhumiputra are of a more permanent nature. Thus these provisions and the one which enshrines Islam as the state religion in such a pluralistic and numerically well-poised population has the potential for creating an explosive situation in the long term.

The demographic patterns in Sarawak are even more complex. There the Malay/Muslim group is not the dominant majority as in Malaysia. There are numerous tribal indigenous groups in Sarawak and unlike the Orang Asli (indigenous people) of the peninsula who are quite marginal in the demographic structure, they have substantial populations. As a matter of fact, the tribal group of the Iban is the largest ethnic group of Sarawak constituting 31.1% of the population (1970 census). A substantial number of them are Christians and the vast majority follow their traditional animistic religions, beliefs and practices. Nor do Muslims form the dominant religious group there, being only 26.3% of the population, less than the Christians who constitute 28.5% of the population. The Malays of Sarawak form only 19% of the population though they are usually clubbed with the Melanau tribal group, a large number of whom are Muslims, bringing up their combined strength to 25% (1970 census), which still falls short of the Iban total of 31.1%. Population figures also show that the Chinese (30.1%) are in a much stronger position in Sarawak compared to the peninsula, being next to the Ibans in numerical strength and larger than the Malay/Melanau coalition. It is also significant that Sarawak, unlike all other states of the Malaysian federation, has not adopted Islam as the state religion.

In this context Christian-Muslim relations assume quite a different character in Sarawak as compared to the peninsula. This is however not to state that Christian-Muslim relations are much more harmonious in Sarawak. It would be natural to assume that the demographic patterns would ensure that the Christians (28.5% in Sarawak as opposed to 8.6% for the whole federation), would be in a much stronger position to argue for and achieve rights and privileges However past experience and my own conversations with Christians in Sarawak have not indicated this to be the case.

In spite of its numerically less preponderant position in Sarawak, the Malay/Melanau group has in recent times dominated the political scene in Sarawak and has led the state coalition governments. The intervention of the UMNO led Federal

Government has been a very important factor in the state politics, with financial patronage and investment of federal funds in projects, issue of licences for timber felling etc. being inducements to various political groups to support the Malay/Melanau leadership group. The Chief Minister, always a Muslim, has deftly manipulated the various political parties and was able to secure a majority in the Sarawak Dewan Undangan Negri (State Parliament) with Chinese and Iban and other indigenous political groupings allying with their Partai Pesaka Bhumiputra Persatu political party. In spite of their numerical strength the indigenous groups were divided and not properly mobilised. Of late a union of various indigenous groups known as the PBDS has tried to mobilise the Sarawak tribal communities and caused the Barisan National (National Front) coalition government much apprehension at the time of elections. Ultimately the BN won through in the 1991 elections, but with a reduced majority. The BN characterised the opposition as racist, (though their manifesto reflects a more egalitarian ideology than that of the ruling National Front), and their own alliance as multi-racial. But whether its actions have always been multi-racial and egalitarian is a disputable point in view of the allegations by the Christians and other groups there. As later discussions of my researches in Sarawak tend to show there are considerable misgivings among the Christians regarding the privileged and dominant position of the Malay/Muslim group in Sarawak, as on the peninsula, in spite of the entirely different demographic patterns of the state. It is true that the indigenous groups have not benefitted adequately from the rich resources of oil, gas and timber of the state. There has been an allegation that the former Chief minister had sold to PETRONAS, a peninsular Oil Corporation, Sarawak petroleum at a much cheaper rate than could have been normally obtained,(2) thus affecting substantially the revenues due to the state. Very little of the profits from timber sales, the second largest Malaysian export after petroleum, has trickled down to the indigenous inhabitants of the forestry areas. It is said that the former Governor and his nephew, the present Chief minister, together held licenses for felling 30% of Sarawak forest land (3)- this in spite of a provision in the Sarawak constitution prohibiting the Yang di Pertuan Negeri (State Governor) from engaging in commercial enterprise. [Sarawak Constitution

Article 2(2)] The profits from timber is said to benefit only politicians, a few ex- senior civil servants and their friends and relatives in addition to the logging operators who are predominantly Chinese. The forest dwellers on the other hand, is adversely affected by timber felling, with the loss of habitat of the flora and fauna which form the source of their livelihood.

Although in Sarawak the Federal Government cannot utilise federal funds for the promotion of Islamic institutions they are however channeling funds for this purpose from the state lotteries, a contradiction in terms since Islam is highly opposed to gambling. In spite of its divergent ethnic and religious composition the general policies of Peninsular Malaysia seem to be extant in Sarawak as also the discontentment of the non-Malay/ non-Muslim groups. The chief ministers have usually been proteges of the Federal Government and like the present incumbent, Taib Mohammed, have served for long periods in the federal cabinet and thus become attuned to and in favour of policies formulated in Kuala Lumpur. Thus the distinctiveness which should have arisen from Sarawak's special demographic character has not materialised.

Islam and Christianity are two faiths which have much in common. Both worship virtually the same God, the God of Abraham, Isaac and Jacob, though there are contrasts in their respective understanding of the nature of the Divinity. Islam accepts the Judaic and Christian scriptures as authentic with certain reservations (Tahrif) and agrees with the doctrines of creation, bodily resurrection and final judgement. Jesus is a highly venerated figure in Islam and according to the Qur'an and the Hadith performs greater miracles (e.g. creation of life) than in the Biblical accounts. The Qur'an depicts Christians as the most dear to Muslims among the *Ahl-al-Kitab* (the people who share common scriptures).(4)

In spite of a long history of conflict in ancient and medieval times, there is much potential for harmony between these two faiths. One source of controversy is the fact that both are keen proselytising religions and can and has competed for adherents, but in Malaysia this has been affected by two factors. One is that Islam in Malaysia has not until fairly recently been very active in evangelisation. Secondly, there is a virtual prohibition on Christian and other evangelisation among the Muslims, but not vice versa. This leaves the Muslims at a distinct advantage and there have been attempts by the Malay/ Muslim administrations to change the religious composition of the populations in East Malaysia, particularly in the State of Sabah. Both Sarawak and Sabah had stipulated that a condition for cession with the federation would be that Islam will not be imposed as the state religion. Sarawak has maintained this position though Article 4A (2) of the State Constitution does provide for a council to advise the Yang di Pertuan Agong, (Supreme head of the Malaysian nation, who in Sarawak is the Head of the Religion of Islam while in other states the respective Sultans hold this function). However in 1973 under pressure from the Federal Government Sabah revoked this condition and adopted Islam as the official state religion. Perhaps in conformity with this new status of Islam the Sabah administration led by Muslims have embarked on an aggressive campaign of proselytisation converting large numbers to Islam. It is claimed that during Chief Minister Tun Mustapha's regime (1967-1975), 95000 non-Muslims had been converted, including the leader of the Kadazan native tribe, Donald Stephens, a Christian who took the name Mohammed Fahd. It is stated that access to political power, jobs and government contracts were held out as inducements for conversion. The majority of the indigenous group of Sabah, the Kadazans, a number of whom are Catholics were dismayed by these developments. Happily such aggressive proselytisation was not pursued by the later regimes. Reverend Aries, Principal of the Kuching Theological College whom I interviewed said Islamic revivalist and evangelistic organisations such as BINA are quite discreet in their proselytising activities, probably in deference to the restrictions placed on evangelisation by other religions among Muslims. However the BINA brochure talks of success in conversions.(5) Generally the domination of the political scene by a relative minority section of Malays / Muslims supported by the Federal administration seems to have created much apprehension in Eastern Malaysia among other ethnic groups, the Christians etc.

The modern phenomenon of Islamic revival has not left Malaysia alone. Traditionally Malaysian Islam has tended to be a liberal one, integrating well with the pre-Islamic practices and ritual, a happy combination of Indic, Buddhist and animistic traditions with Islam.

Clifford Geertz in his classic *Religion of Java* gives a colourful account of the highly syncretistic forms that Islam could take in the Malay Archipelago, with feasts to local spirits (*Slametan*), magical practices, divination, and shadow plays from Hindu epics and Buddha statues freely part of Muslim praxis in the region. (6) Part of the reason is that Islam was brought to these parts from Southern Arabia and Western India not by very rigourous or fundamentalist Muslims, but by Sufis who were doctrinally and ritually liberal and always adapted well to local beliefs and traditions. But in recent times as a result of better travel facilities to Arabia and other parts of the Western world, mainly a consequence of the colonial occupation, Muslims from Malaysia have become acquainted with a more rigourous and purist type of Islam, such as the one practiced by Muslims of Iran or Saudi Arabia. The writings of the Islamic Brotherhood of Egypt in their journal *al Manar*, and other tenets of Wahabi ideology propagated by modernists such as Muhammad Abdu and Rashid Rida became influential among the Malaysian urban young, the Kuam Muda. This was a return to an extremely stricter but more rationalistic form of Islam, abjuring syncretism and superstitious practices, such as divination, also much of the ceremonial of local traditions which they look upon as *bida-* innovation. A more individualistic and analytical interpretation of Islam (*ijtihad*) based on the Qur'an and Hadith is advocated, rather than one based on tradition and the consensus of the Ulama. I have attempted to explain in Chapter 4 more fully the reasons for a global Islamic resurgence and for the Malaysian variant. The anti Western, anti-secularist and anti-Zionist characteristics of the revival is visible in Malaysia as in all Islamic countries where such fundamentalistic resurgence is taking place. Its appeal has strangely been among the more educated and urban middle classes, and to some extent the old guard in rural Malaysia, the Kuam Tua are wary of and hostile to these developments. The sad fact remains that though this revival is known as modernist it is far from progressive. It is essentially backward-looking and is unable to reconcile itself to the modern context and suffers from serious tensions between its call to revert to the 7th century situation of the Prophet's time in Arabia and its ideals, and the realities of modern life. However the activities of PERMAS, Dar al Arqam, the Jamaat- I - Tabligh and other revivalist organisations have had a significant impact on Malay politics and more seriously on inter- religious relations. The father of the Nation, Tunku Abdul Rahman and even the modern leaders such as Mahathir Muhammad and Taib Mohammed of Sarawak have serious reservations about the viability of the revivalist ideology and its exhortation for a full- fledged Islamic state, where the Sharia would be strictly and universally implemented. At the 11th annual meeting of BINA at Kuching, in Sept 1963 the Chief Minister reminded Muslims that there is no compulsion in religion and that Muslims should keep abreast with the challenges of the times, a subtle hint that revival should be dynamic, progressive and gentle, not backward looking, retrogressive and coercive. (7)

Dr. Mahathir reiterates in *The Challenge* a similar policy towards Islamic revival, and decries extremism, citing the case of Egypt where fundamentalists are ready to assassinate Muslim leaders and exhort government officials to disobey them.(8) In recent times the emphasis on Malay ethnicity seems to have shifted to the Islamic identity, though the Malay- Muslim equation and the exclusion of non- Malay Muslims from Bhumiputra status serve to ensure the predominance of Malay identity in the consciousness of the majority group. Though the Tunku had categorically stated that Malaysia is not a Muslim state and that other religions have total freedom of worship, inevitably the administrations have had to take cognizance of the appeal that Islamic revival has on the masses, and more dangerously on the educated and youthful elite, no doubt the pillars of the future, and has had to out manoeuvre fundamentalist organisations such as PAS with their own pro- Islamic measures such as funding of mosques, *sauras* (prayer houses), *madrasas* (religious schools) and *dawah*(revival) organisations and the setting up of an Islamic University, Islamic Bank and international Qur'an reading competition. The advantage to the nation as a whole of the latter two organisations is quite dubious. It has to be stated that the use of state funds on one particular religion seems to be rather unjust and discriminatory in a democracy, especially one which is as multi-faith as Malaysia. In Sarawak the preponderance of the Christian faith 28.5% (1980 census) as opposed to the Muslim(26.3%) and the existence of substantial proportions of Buddhist, Confucian, Indian and tribal religions would mean that the *dawah* movement and especially the state government's support for it have to be more circumspect. The Minister for Industrial Development, Haji Openg, stated that the state government will strive for continued progress and development of the *rakyat* (the proletariat) irrespective of their racial origins or religious beliefs.[9] However, according to the Sarawak Gazette of July 1991, the same minister seems to state on 25th April that Sarawak will be the first state in Malaysia to implement the Shariah for Muslims.

The Malaysian constitution has extended the special privileges enjoyed by the Malays to the Bhumiputra. While this has very little significance in the peninsula where the indigenous tribes such as the Orang Asli are marginal, in Sarawak, where non-Malay natives are the majority, this provision has a significant impact. However, in spite of these provisions, Christians in Sarawak, the vast number of whom are Ibans, who are Bhumiputra and eligible for privileges, state that discrimination in favour of the Muslims still exist. I interviewed Charles Saong, a senior official of the Dewan Bahasa Dan Pustaka organisation, a government establishment for the promotion and regulation of Malaysian language and literature. In spite of his long experience and high seniority in the organisation he said that he had been superseded by a young Malay/Muslim. According to Charles his experience of discrimination and consequent frustrations is quite common among Christian employees especially in the public sector. The extension of privileges to the Bhumiputra, many of whom are tribals, a majority of the forest dwellers among whom are backward in all respects, seems to indicate a genuine desire in the Administration to uplift the backward sections of society. However instances such as that of Charles seem to negate the impact and effectiveness of the implementation of these policies. I put this question to Colonel Dunstan Nynaring, a political secretary to the Chief Minister, a brilliant former military officer and diplomat. Colonel Dunstan seemed to be rather to conciliatory to the Muslim politicians stating that it was usual for administrators in the top echelons of the bureaucracy to have people whom they could trust in key positions. He thus seems to condone some kind of informal networking, a sort of Malay/Muslim caucus in the administration. According to him this was not the result of a significant governmental policy. But such favouritism and discrimination among the Malay/Bhumiputra sector would lead to further imbalances in society already to some extent aggravated by the apparent Muslim resurgence and domination

In the matter of day-to-day religious practice the Malaysian constitution accords perfect freedom to all citizens. However the reality seems to be somewhat less ideal than this. Dr. Tan Chee Khoon in a strong and forthright article in *Constitutional Provisions for Religious Freedom in Malaysia* lists several incidents that seem to undermine the correctness and fairness of the constitutional provision. He accepts the special status of Islam in the nation and the prohibition of proselytisation among Muslims, in spite of some earlier reservations. However he points to the difficulties posed by Muslim organisations and bureaucrats over the establishment of a church in Subang Jaya, the general aversion to the proximity of churches to mosques, (a common phenomenon in Indonesia, where many churches and mosques exist side by side without engendering any hostility), the ban on placing Bibles in hotels by the Gideons, (again permitted in Indonesia), the paucity of Christian programmes in the media at Christmas etc., which seem to indicate an innate hostility to the Christian faith.[10] There is no overt or blatant persecution, but as Rev. Aries states there are tendencies which point to a more subtle but nevertheless worrying forms of oppression.

Education is not only a vital sector of corporate life, but a significant factor in the development of future attitudes and perspectives of the populace. In Sarawak, as in many other regions of Malaysia the western mode of education was initiated during the colonial times by Christian missions who established schools with a view to both propagating the Christian faith, as also to "civilise" the natives, which in effect meant changing their culture to conform with the western cultural garb of the Christianity which they brought to the Eastern world. This two-pronged strategy was however counter-productive in that many of the Easterners tended to view Christianity as a Western religion, though its origins were Semitic and Asian rather than European. The fact however remains that the missionaries were well-intentioned and gave the Malaysians an opportunity to learn English and become eligible for whatever positions were offered them in the colonial administration, not to speak of the long-term benefits of opening to them a bridge to the

Western world and its scientific and technological achievements. In Sarawak, the Brooke administrations were not much enamoured of westernising the populace, but looked upon western education as a useful tool for the material advancement of the people. After *Merdeka* the Malaysian administrations rightly sought to reform the Western orientation of the educational system and make it more attuned to the ethos of the nation. But as in other spheres the dominance of the Malay/ Muslim culture is visible in the reformed schools, to some extent ignoring the pluralistic nature of Malaysian society. Thus, there is considerable dissatisfaction among the non-Malay/non-Muslim sections of the populace. The promotion of Bahasa Malaysia (the Malay language) is in some ways a legitimate move since national integration and unity should be an objective of education and this cannot be achieved until there is a common means of communication in the country. However this need not be at the expense of other languages such as Chinese, or in Sarawak, Iban. Linguistic controversies abound in India and Pakistan regarding the status of Hindi/Urdu vis-a-vis minority languages, but in Malaysia, where the minorities are not vastly inferior numerically to the majority, sufficient consideration has to be given to their languages. Similarly while elements of the Islamic faith are taught to Muslim students there is no provision for the teaching of other faiths during school hours even in Christian schools. Teachers in aided schools cannot teach non- Muslims religious instruction even on a purely voluntary and honorary basis. Islamic history is a mandatory subject in all teacher-training institutions, thus providing the future pedagogues an understanding of and perhaps affinity with Islam, a salutary consequence no doubt, but one which could have been supplemented by acquaintance with the Christian, Buddhist, Hindu and other major faiths of the nation. In Sarawak, knowledge of Iban, Bidayuh and other tribal religions would be quite useful to teachers who potentially could be working in areas where the people following indigenous religion would be in a majority. Government policy thus seems to be promoting the study of Islam, while discouraging knowledge of other faiths. This certainly is not conducive to national integration or religious harmony.

Perhaps due to these imbalances in religious instruction Muslim educational authorities were quite reluctant to talk to me about these issues. Was it a guilty conscience or was it merely reluctance to discuss sensitive issues with a foreigner? The Head of a state school whom I tried to meet was almost discourteous in her efforts to put me off, and a Malay/Muslim Education officer whom I met told me I had to receive permission from Kuala Lumpur to talk to him. He finally relented and did give me an interview. He presented a picture of much religious tolerance in education at least in the secondary level sector, that he was concerned with. He told me that he himself had taught Christian knowledge (sic) in a mission school that he had visited on his inspection tour. If this is true the prohibition of the inclusion of non-Muslim faiths that Gordon P. Means mentions is not applicable to Sarawak. Roy Bruton in his book on education in Sarawak does mention Bible knowledge as one of the optional subjects for the Sarawak Junior School Certificate Examination (SJSCE) (though it was not included when the syllabus was brought into conformity with the national syllabi LCE) in 1991.[11] Similarly, in the senior MCE (Malaysian Certificate of Education), while Islamic studies is one of the possible options there is no mention of instruction in other faiths in the prescribed syllabus.[12]

Tertiary education is a vital factor for personal success in Malaysia. Here also the state had been empowered by a constitutional amendment to give special reservations for Malays/Bhumiputra in courses at Universities. This prerogative extends to the grant of overseas scholarships.

The Federal Government has made public discussion of sensitive issues illegal, and since inter-ethnic and inter-religious relations fall into this category, the ethnic and religious minorities are quite restricted in opposing injustices and imbalances against their rights, a point which came up often in my conversations with Christians in Sarawak. In 1971, when emergency rule which followed the racial riots of May 1969 ended, the Abdul Razak administration introduced a whole package of constitutional amendments limiting freedom of speech and the press on issues such as the special status of Malays and the religion of Islam. While there is certainly a need to prevent scurrilous or defamatory propaganda which might foment racial and religious hatred, these provisions could very well be misused by a party in power to stifle criticism and even the airing of legitimate grievances by minorities, the opposition, or victims of oppression. As Gordon P. Means graphically describes, Dr. Mahathir has also mounted a campaign against the judiciary culminating in the dismissal of the Chief Justice of the Supreme Court, Salah Abbas and some other judges and the introduction of amendments to the constitution impairing judicial authority and judicial review. [13] The independence of the judiciary is vital for any democracy, as it is often the last resort for redress of grievances for victims of injustice and oppression, and the paramount seat of power in public administration, often overriding even parliament if its activities infringed the letter or the spirit of the national constitution. In many third world countries where there is potential for corruption even in the highest echelons of political and bureaucratic centres of power, the integrity and independence of the judiciary is sometimes the only factor preventing total disruption. The trial of Mrs. Gandhi, the Indian Prime Minister for electoral malpractices is an instance to the point. The restrictions on the fundamental human rights of freedom of expression and association (e. g. The Societies Act empowering the Registrar of Societies to deregister organisations), and the impairment of judicial authority and independence of the legal system, constitute a grave threat to human rights and democracy in Malaysia. As Gordon P. Means remarks, whereas in most parts of the world there is an enhancement of freedom and human rights, in Malaysia the tendency is in the opposite direction.[14] Much of the deterioration in democratic and fundamental rights seems to be related to the question of ethnic and religious issues, namely the special status of the Malay/ Muslim.

References

1. For instance, Dr. Tan Chee Beng (1985), See, Khoon, Tan Chee, *Malaysia Today*, Pelanduk Publications: Petaling Jeya , p. 25.
2. Bruton, Roy (1993), *Farewell to Democracy in Sarawak*, Merlin Books: Braunton, Devon, p. 239.
3. Chin, S.C., Devaraj, J., and Jin, K.K. (1989) *Logging against the Natives of Sarwak*, Insan, (Institute of Social Analysis), p. viii.

4. Qur'an 5:82.

5. Angkatan Nahadathul Islam Bersatu (United Islamic Renaissance Movement) (1993), *BINA, A Brief Introduction*, BINA: Kuching, p. 8.

6. See Geertz, C., *Religion of Java*, and *Islam Observed*.

7. *Sunday Tribune*, 18th September 1993.

8. Mohammed, Mahathir (1986), *The Challenge*, Pelanduk Publications: Petaling Jeya, p.105.

9. *Sararwak Gazette*, December 1989, p. 52.

10. Khoon, Tan Sri Dr. Chee (1984) "Constitutional Provisions for Religious Freedom", in *Contemporary Issues in Malaysian Religions*, Pelanduk Publications: Petaling Jeya, pp. 18-44, pp. 32&33.

11. Bruton, Roy (1993), *Farewell to Democracy in Sarawak*, Merlin Books Ltd.: Braunton, p. 186.

12. Ibid, p. 190.

13. Means, Gordon P. (1991), *Malaysian Politics- the Second Generation*, Oxford University Press: Singapore, pp. 237-238.

14. Ibid, p.310.

2 Islam and Christianity - some reflections

The Semitic religions of Judaism, Christianity and Islam have close historical and doctrinal roots. These faiths are sometimes termed the Abrahamic faiths, since Abraham is an important figure for all three. Indeed Abraham is a patriarch of the founders of all three religions. Abraham is Israel's grandfather. The Gospel of Matthew provides a detailed genealogy of Jesus, tracing his ancestry to Abraham through Isaac. (Matthew Ch. 1) Muslims look upon Abraham as their ancestor through his son Ishmael. The Qur'an affirms this, when it states:

> He has chosen you, and has imposed no difficulties on you in religion; it is the cult of your father Abraham.(Sura 22:78)

Thus not only was Abraham the ancestor of Muhammad but the latter was following the creed that Abraham himself held.

In other words, Islam is nothing but the religion followed by Abraham.

As a matter of fact Islam looks upon Abraham as the first Muslim in the literal sense of one who submits to God. They point out that Abraham was neither a Jew nor a Christian, the patriarch preceding these appellations by several generations.

The central figures of Christianity and Islam, namely Jesus and Muhammad are thus both claimed to be descendants of Abraham. The Abrahamic salt no doubt will preserve the commonality of these three religious traditions.

Doctrinally and ritualistically Islam is much closer to Judaism than to Christianity. The strong monotheism of its faith (as opposed to the qualified monotheism of the Christian Trinity), its emphasis on rituals - "the five pillars of Islam" and the law, is reminiscent more of Judaism than Christianity. However, Islam has always had a special place in its affection for the Christians. This is especially true of the modern context when the relations between Muslims and Christians are much more harmonious than of the former with the Jews. The Qur'an itself reiterates this affinity with the statement.

> Strongest among men in enmity
> To the Believers wilt thou
> Find the Jews and pagans;
> And nearest among them in love
> To the believers wilt thou
> find those who say
> "We are Christians" (Sura 5:85)

One of the reasons adduced by the Qur'an for this affinity is the Christians' humility and lack of arrogance, probably as contrasted with Jewish pride and exclusiveness. (Sura 5:85). This may be so, but it definitely has in addition some historical rationale harking back to the times of prophet Muhammad .

Firstly it should be remembered that at the height of the persecution by the Quraysh it was a Christian king, the Negus of Abbyssinia (modern Ethiopia) who gave refuge to the Muslims fleeing from Mecca. Secondly, Yathrib or Madina (complete name Madinat al Nabi -- City of the Prophet), the first Islamic state, had a number of Jewish inhabitants, who were given equal rights with Muslim citizens by the Prophet. As a matter of fact the Prophet considered the Jews and Christians of Madina to be fellow Muslims. However the Jews of Madina did not fully reciprocate Muhammad's overtures of friendship. Significantly they poured ridicule on Muhammad's teachings based on the revelations of the Qur'an, pointing out the discrepancies between these and their own beliefs. These were certainly not vast in comparison to that of the Quraysh, and certainly not an insurmountable obstacle for rapprochement between Jews and Muslims, but the Jews took a very hard and perhaps superior attitude, and were inclined to categorise Muhammad as an impostor. This may be why the Qur'an implies that the Jews were arrogant. Even more seriously, some of them passed secret information to the Quraysh, the enemies of Islam. Eventually Muhammad banished many of the Jewish tribes from Madeena, and later even executed substantial numbers of them for treason, though the actual decision for putting the Jews to death was taken not by the Prophet himself, but by Sa'd Ibn Muadh, one of the *Ansar* (helpers), the original residents of Madina.

In spite of the good scriptural basis for harmonious relations, the history of Christian-Muslim relations has been plagued by controversies, dissension and wars over the centuries. The conquest and reconquest of Spain, the Crusades, the rivalry between Muslims and the Portuguese in Western India, and more recently the conflict in Lebanon are examples of Christian-Muslim conflict at the level of armed combat. Christian-Muslim polemics of a less aggressive but however sometimes quite virulent nature, has been a perennial feature of the history of relations between the two faiths. In medieval days such controversies were vitiated by the fact that both religions did not take the pains for an authentic understanding of the beliefs and practices of each other. Before the 12th century the depiction of Islam by Christian writers, for example St. John of Damascus, was full of misconceptions and distortions of the reality. Many lowered Islam to the status of a Christian heresy. Stories abounded of Muslims worshipping Muhammad and idols, such as that of Aphrodite, of the Prophet receiving revelations from a dove perched on his shoulder, and of being finally eaten up by pigs! Muslim writers tended to view Christianity as being arrantly polytheistic, charging that Christians worshipped God, Jesus and Mary! The doctrine of *Tahrif* (changing of the scriptures) based on the Qur'an explained away the discrepancies between the Qur'an and the Christian scriptures such as the doctrine of the Trinity and Jesus' death on the cross. The doctrine of *Tahrif* charges that the Jewish and Christian scriptures have changed in the course of time and have even been deliberately distorted to substantiate such Christian doctrines. It claims that Jesus foretold the coming of Muhammad, a prophecy which has been concealed by the writers of the Gospels. The doctrine of *Tahrif* uses terms such as *tabdil* (substitution), *misyan* (forgetfulness), *kitman* (concealing the text) and *lawa* (mispronunciation). Books were supposed to have been delivered to Moses, David and Jesus from heaven, just as the Qur'an to Muhammad, but were lost, forgotten, changed or misinterpreted by the Christians and Jews. Jesus is stated to have prophesied the coming of Prophet Muhammad, but the present text of the Gospels make no mention of this prophecy, substituting instead the coming of the Holy Spirit, the *Paraklytos* instead of the *Periklytos* (The Praised One or Muhammad).

As a matter of fact there is much potential on a purely religious basis for dialogue and amity between Christians and Muslims. There is no doubt that all three Abrahamic faiths worship the same being, be it called Yahweh, God or Allah. The God of Abraham, Isaac and Jacob is the Deity worshipped by Muslims. They believe in a creator God and that he created the human being in His image. The creative process described in the Qur'an (through the word *kun* -let it be) is essentially the same as in the Christian scriptures. There are however differences in the understanding of the nature of God. Judaism emphasises a God who is just and mighty. Christians talk of the fatherly love of God, rather than his power or justice. Islam emphasises God's glory, power and transcendence. Nevertheless, Islam also believes in a God who is *al Rahman*, and *al Rahim*, the Merciful and the Compassionate, one who has created the world, is desirous of saving us from hell, and is holy, concepts which are not far removed from the Christian understanding of God. The Book of Revelation in the Christian Bible also talks unceasingly of God's glory, his wrath and vengeance on sinners. Thus the concept of God in the two faiths are not as disparate as seems at a first glance. Christians believe in a God, who as the indwelling Holy Spirit is close to us. The Qur'an states:

> It was we who
> Created man, and we know
> What dark suggestions his soul

Makes to him; for We
Are nearer to him
Than his jugular vein

(Sura 50:16)

This suggests a God who is immanent as well as transcendent.

Muslims as Christians believe in the physical resurrection of the dead at the end of time, the judgement of all human beings and rewards in heaven for the virtuous and punishment in hell for the wicked. Muslims acknowledge the virgin birth of Christ, call him *al Masih*, the Messiah, and believe in Jesus's miracles. As a matter of fact the Qur'an depicts Jesus as a much more exalted figure than Prophet Muhammad. The miracle of speaking from the cradle, and that of creating life(birds from clay), narrated in the Qur'an are not recounted in the canonical gospels. (Sura 19:30 and Sura 5:113) The Qur'an talks of Christ as a sign and a word from God (Sura, 23:50 and 4:171) These are only some of the numerous ways in which the two faiths converge in their portrayal of Jesus. Thus though Islam denies the divinity of Jesus, the Qur'an acknowledges God-like powers in Jesus, far greater than those implied in the Gospel miracles.

Both Islam and Christianity are seen to be involved in reforming earlier religious traditions. Jesus stated that he came to confirm the law and the prophets, but engaged in a radical reinterpretation of Jewish beliefs and practices, restoring the lost inner reality and spiritual significance of God's commandments. Muhammad battled against the excessive idolatry, polytheism and commercialisation of the religious tradition of Mecca. Both were highly critical of the religious authorities of the day and were consequently persecuted by them. Muhammad almost lost his life shortly before his emigration to Yathrib, the *Hijra*, and Jesus was crucified (according to Christians) by the Romans at the instigation of Jewish religious leaders.

Both Islam and Christianity represent a movement away from narrow tribalism and regionalism. Christianity transcended the exclusiveness of Judaism, and spread to the Mediterranean nations and eventually world wide, not without some soul searching by the early Christians. The controversy between Paul and some of Christ's disciples on the issue of Jews and gentiles is testimony to the difficulties that the Christian faith had in its movement towards universality.(1) Islam unified the Arabs abolishing their tribalism and the perennial feuds, raids (*razzia*), warring and fragmentation of Arab society, and then spread far beyond Arabia at a rapid pace, embracing people of all races, colours and nations. Both are keen proselytising religions, and the initial phenomenal expansion of both continues to some extent even in modern times.

In spite of these similarities there are areas of disagreement and contrast in the two faiths which can constitute the greatest obstacles for dialogue and rapprochement. We will examine these issues in some detail one by one.

The understanding of God in Islam and Christianity

Muslims use the term *Allah* for God, a word which simply means the God (*al Ilah*). The use of the definitive singular reveals the strong monotheistic faith of Islam - there can be no other gods but Allah. They like Christians visualise God in mainly anthropomorphic terms, and speak of the body of God, his head and his feet etc. The Qur'an for instance states, "So glory be to Him in whose hand is the kingdom of all things" (Sura 38:75) and "Which swims forth under Our eye" (Sura 64:14)

But the great Turkish Muslim philosopher al Farabi opined that there is no genus under which God could be subsumed.(2) He is above all such distinctions. The Mutazila considered such statements as metaphorical expressions. They rejected a literal understanding of such statements. Muslims will never use the term *father* for God. Use of terms such as *father*, which denote human relationships is obnoxious to the Muslim, so great is their preoccupation with the exaltation, majesty and transcendence of God. To use such terms as *father* would be to them an act of irreverence. However every Sura (chapter) of the Qur'an begins with the declaration: "In the name of God the merciful, the compassionate".

The Sufi tradition in Islam is close to the Christian understanding and cites texts such as "God is closer to one than the vein in the neck" (Sura 50:16, 2:186) which speak of God's nearness to the human being, and suggests His immanence in addition to his transcendence. Celebrated Sufis such as Rabiya al Adawiya emphasised the mutual love between Allah and the devotee, a concept not stressed in conventional Islam. Also the very fact that Allah is desirous of reaching out to humanity and to save them through books and messengers testifies to His love, a point of convergence with Christian notions of God.

What is a more serious divergence is the Christian concept of Trinity. Islam has almost an obsession with monotheism, even to the extent that it is reluctant to speak of God's qualities to avoid any kind of personification of God's attributes, leading to what they fear would be polytheism. The Mutazilites, the Unitarians *par excellence* of Islam would say that 'God knows', 'God is powerful' and so on, rather than state that God possesses knowledge, power, etc. They were apprehensive of the hypostatisation of God's qualities into other divinities. The Druze, one of the Shiite sects Lebanon and Syria have such concepts. They believe God's attributes have incarnated into the world as different beings. These are the Universal Intelligence, the Universal Soul, the Word, the Right Wing and the Left Wing. The Muslims say this is what has happened in the Christian faith, where the Word of God and His Spirit have become gods along with God the Father. They would evidently consider the Trinity to include such personifications, e.g. the idea of *Logos*, Jesus as the Word of God, and the Holy Spirit, the spirit of God. For Muslims God is *wahid* - his essence is absolutely one, He is indivisible. Historically the controversies of Muhammad with the Quray'sh related mainly to questions of God's *wahadat*, his uniqueness, and the main thrust of Muhammad's mission in Mecca was the eradication of polytheism.

Jesus

The status of Jesus is closely linked to this issue. To the Christian Jesus is Son of God, part of the Godhead, member of the Trinity. To

Islam he is human, though a highly exalted prophet and messenger who was given the *Injil*, the Gospel, a book brought down from heaven by archangel Gabriel. To equate anyone with God or to speak of a filial relationship with God which goes beyond the metaphorical, is *bida*, innovation, and *shirk*, ascribing partners to God, serious sins. *Shirk* is spoken of as the unforgivable sin in Islam. In the Qur'an Jesus himself disclaims that he is God or the Son of God. But the Qur'an itself uses the terms *word, spirit and sign* for Jesus (Sura 4:171, 43:61), words which echo the Christian conception of Jesus. But Islam has some deep-rooted objections to the idea of the incarnation of God. The world is too impure and imperfect for God to dwell in. God is too exalted and glorious to take human form. Incarnation compromises the unity of God. The great Muslim theologian al Ghazzali exclaimed that the Christians believe that Allah died on the cross and there was no Creator in heaven for three days. Muslims argue that God is omnipotent and can save the world by a fiat of His will. Thus there is no need for the incarnation. Christians argue that the coming of Yahweh in person to deliver his people is foretold by prophets (as in Isaiah, 11:16 and 31 and in Jeremiah 14: 8.) Genesis 3:15 states that the seed of a woman will bruise the serpent, implying that the vanquishing of the devil will be performed by a man, i.e. God in human form. Jesus spoke many a time of his unity with God the Father.[3] Jesus's miracles and the acknowledgement of his disciples who were close to him and witnessed his transfiguration on the mountain near Bethsaida, and called him *Kyrios* seem to testify to the fact that he was more than human.

Ontological issues related to the Trinity and especially Jesus has been hotly debated ever since the formulation of the doctrine in the 2nd to 4th centuries. Differences in the understanding of the Trinity, especially the status of the Holy Spirit separated the Eastern and Western churches. In the Deistic atmosphere of the 18th century the doctrine suffered almost an eclipse and there was a rise in Unitarian views of God. However in the twentieth century belief in the Trinity was re-established in most churches mainly due to the efforts of Karl Barth. There was also considerable speculation as to the nature and status of Jesus, and many divergent views from the orthodox conception enshrined in the Athanasian, Chalcedonian and Nicene creeds, such as Arianism, Monarchianism, Monophysitism, and Adoptionism were extant until the controversies were settled and to some extent stifled by the Councils of Chalcedon and Nicea in the 4th century. But the debate on Jesus goes on, and the controversial views of theologians such as Bultmann and Schweitzer, and works such as *The Myth of God Incarnate* (4), testify to the fact that the debate on Jesus is certainly not at an end. It is then no wonder that a strongly monotheistic faith such as Islam should have reservations about the divinity of Jesus and his sonship to God.

Though Islam believes that Jesus was merely a man, but also a highly exalted prophet, and had no part of the divine in Him, the Qur'anic depiction of Jesus does make him a highly supernatural figure, endowed with God-like powers. Jesus, for instance, speaks as an infant to the Jews soon after his birth, defending Mary when they accused Mary of adultery (Sura 3:48). The most significant miracle is the creation of live pigeons from models of clay. Jesus fashioned the birds out of clay and blew in to them when they became alive and flew away. The process of fashioning from clay and breathing life in to them is highly reminiscent of God's creation of Man in Genesis Chapter 2. In the Qur'an thus Jesus is the creator of life, not just the restorer of life as in the canonical Gospel accounts of the raising of Lazarus and the widow's son. It must be remembered that similar acts of raising the dead were performed by some of the Apostles in later times.

The nature of revelation in Christianity and Islam

Islam as Christianity believes that God has constantly been trying to reveal himself to humanity, through prophets, scriptures and great works of a miraculous nature. Islam believes that before the fall of man, humanity had perfect and spontaneous knowledge of God. Expelling the primal human beings from the Garden of Eden God told them that they will lose this innate knowledge of Him, but that he will from time to time be sending prophets and messengers with holy books relating to humanity knowledge of His nature, his will and his plan for the world. Islam believes that a book thus sent through the Prophet Ibrahim (Abraham) has been lost. The prophets

Musa, (Moses), Dawood (David), and Isa (Jesus) brought respectively the books, the *Tawrat* (Torah) the *Dabur* (The Book of Psalms) and the *Injil* (Evangel or the Gospel) These are excerpts from the great book, the "Well-guarded Tablet", set near the throne of God and co-eternal with Him. (Some sectarian groups such as the Mutazila--now extinct-- and the Shia oppose this belief in the eternity of the Qur'an). The final book sent through the final prophet, Muhammad, the *khatm* (seal) of the prophets is the Qur'an, the most perfectly preserved revelation from God.

The Qur'an as well as the Christian scriptures speak of the revelation of God in nature. (Ps. 19, Romans 1:20, Sura 21:41-45, and 78:6-16 for example). But to Christians the supreme revelation of God is Jesus himself. In his behaviour, words and actions Jesus reveals, in a most humanly perceptible and to Christians historically authenticated way, the nature of God. Trinitarian theology which believes in the identity of the Son with the Father supports this view of God revealing himself through His son. Thus in Christianity revelation is a presence, while in Islam it is primarily an auditory experience. The Qur'an literally means recitation, and it is through the recitation of God's word that He communicates himself. This is transmitted orally and later on set down in parchments. Thus the text of the Qur'an is infallible, unchanged, untranslatable and unchallenged. There is no discipline of textual and other forms of criticism of the Qur'an as exists in the Biblical scholarly tradition. Disbelief in the Qur'an is a grave sin. The Qur'an is highly revered and is never set on the ground, or placed under other books in a pile.

Christians have a different perception of the communication of revelation. Though they believe in the ultimate inspired nature of their scriptures they do admit a sentient role and involvement of the human authors of these scriptures. The highly literalistic nature of Muslim understanding of scripture as God's word is absent in the Christian attitude to the Bible. Thus the role of language is less critical in Christianity and translations and even recasting of the original sentences, the so called "dynamic equivalents" and paraphrases are permitted. We have thus translations of the Bible into several languages, and various versions each stylistically different and passages with differing theological emphases in differing versions. Muslims cannot condone this. As far as they are concerned there can be only one avenue of communicating God's word -- in the form and language in which it was revealed to the prophet or messenger or whoever was the recipient of the book or recitation from the angel. Recently Islam has relaxed this very rigorous stance and permitted translation of the Qur'an into other languages, probably as a concession to the need for propagation of the faith, but it is significant that the first Muslim translations were brought out by the Ahamadiyyas, a sect perceived as heretical by the orthodoxy. Every Muslim attempts to learn Arabic in order to read the Qur'an in the original, though not all of them are successful to the extent of understanding the complex classical form of the language in which this highly poetic and powerful book has been set down.

The miraculous nature of the Qur'an (indeed Muhammad pointed it out as the only miracle with which he is associated) is augmented considerably by the fact that he was an illiterate. This has the added effect in affirming the Qur'an as wholly God's word, in removing from it any involvement of the Prophet in its composition, since it was manifestly impossible for him to give shape to such beautiful and powerful verse. Non- Muslim scholars have however pointed out that the Prophet may not have been literally illiterate, if such an expression is permissible. The fact of his having been a highly successful merchant and manager of his wife's business supports this premise. Whatever may be the truth we can however point to, in the Christian tradition, apostles such as Peter, the fisherman with little learning or literary background writing epistles of weighty thought and import.

The sinful nature of the human being

Christians believe that the act of disobedience of the first human beings Adam and Eve, symbolically depicted as the eating of the forbidden apple, and their expulsion from the Garden of Eden marks a significant change in human nature, *the fall*, as it is commonly termed. It is believed that this event has caused estrangement between God and humanity, and all human beings are necessarily blighted by this primeval act of sin. Thus everyone is born into the world as a sinner. Islam rejects this notion of "original sin". They believe in the inherently perfect nature of the human being, who is believed to reflect God's glory, though the temptations of the world and evil forces such as Iblis, the Devil are likely to contaminate the human being later. But every child is born a Muslim, one who submits to God, obedient and perfect in nature. Prophets such as Jesus remain sinless throughout their life uncontaminated by Satan or the evils of the world.

Salvation in Islam and Christianity

Islam and Christianity are both salvific religions. Both believe in a God who saves. However the beliefs about the process of salvation is quite different in the two religions. The Christian concept of salvation is an extension of Judaic ideas of piaculatory sacrifice. The Mosaic law specifies in detail the nature and process of sacrifices needed to compensate for sins and to obtain God's forgiveness. The underlying principle is that the wages of sin are death (Romans 6: 23) and that a life is to be given for counteracting the consequences of sin. God is loving and merciful but He is also infinitely perfect and holy and His inexorable and flawless justice requires that sins have to be atoned for before the sinner is exonerated of his misdeeds. The idea of redeeming, i.e. buying back is strong in the Jewish ideology of a life for a life. In Jewish law birds and animals were sacrifices in lieu of the sinner in order that the sacrifier's sins were atoned for. Such piaculatory sacrifices are considered by the Christian as a temporary measure before the advent of Jesus into the world to become the supreme and eternal sacrificial lamb. Christians believe that Jesus bore the sins of the whole world and died on the cross to atone for the sins of humanity, though he himself was perfectly sinless, the unblemished sacrificial lamb. Thus Jesus has saved every one past, present and future. Christ is God, and the infinite nature of His atonement obviates the necessity for further sacrifices of animals or birds which anyway were limited in both their efficacy and duration of effectiveness.

Thus the Christian belief of salvation through the death of Jesus is a natural extension of the idea of vicarious atonement found in the

Jewish religious tradition. Islam differs from this in that they do not believe in the kind of substitution on which Jewish and Christian soteriological beliefs are based. Islam believes in atonement of sins by good deeds carried out by the sinner himself. The Qur'an, the Hadith and the Sharia specifies such good deeds which are efficacious in atoning for sins. The rituals of the *Ibadah* -- Witnessing the faith, Prayer, Almsgiving, Fasting and Pilgrimage are such good deeds, as are reading the Qur'an, and the *dikhr* - remembering God. However good deeds carried out for the sake of others are not unknown in Islam. One can for instance perform the Hajj in lieu of another, who is unable to go on pilgrimage for reasons of health etc. Reading of the Qur'an over the graves of the newly dead is believed to acquire merit for the deceased soul.

However the main emphasis in Islam is piaculatory deeds which can counteract sins and have to be carried out by the sinner him/herself. Christianity however judges good deeds as inefficacious in atoning for sins. They believe humanity to be essentially sinful. "No one does good, no not even one" says St. Paul.(Romans 3:12). Even at birth we are blighted with the original sin of Adam and Eve. Islam does not believe in this. They believe that Adam was not deliberately sinful but was drunk or forgetful of God's commands, and thus was forgiven by God. They believe that every child is born a Muslim into the world, sinless and perfect--the image of God Himself. Christians on the other hand do not believe that but for the redemption of the cross and the work of the Holy Spirit within human beings no one would be saved from God' s punishment. Christ through his death on the cross has reconciled God and the world estranged from Him by sin, symbolised by the tearing of the veil in the Temple at Jerusalem when Jesus died on the cross.

But then Muslims do not believe that Jesus died on the cross. Jesus was taken up bodily into heaven. In the Islamic tradition there are several versions of what happened in Golgotha. The death of Christ on the cross was an illusion created by God to delude the Jews and the Romans. Or someone else was crucified--Judas Iscariot, Jesus Barabbas or Simon the Cyrenean who helped Christ carry the cross. Christ did not die on the cross, but was taken up into heaven in the body. Thus Muslims believe in Jesus's ascension, but not his death and resurrection, two key elements of Christian belief.

Though the perception of Jesus in Islam has these divergences from Christian belief, in the Qur'an itself we come across some statements which seem to approximate more to the Christian belief than orthodox Muslim theologians would allow.

> And remember when the angels said: 'O Mary, Lo! Allah give you glad tidings of a *word* from Him, whose name is the Messiah, Jesus, son of Maryam, *illustrious in this world and the Hereafter*, and *one of those brought near unto Allah'* (italics mine)
>
> Sura 3:48

Some of these statements have echoes of Christian beliefs regarding Jesus' s glory and authority and close relationship to God (sitting at God's right hand) in heaven. Muslims, like Christians, believe in the parousia, the return of Jesus to the world, to conquer evil, though they do not agree with the Christian belief that Jesus will judge the world. In Sura :19: 30 Jesus says:

> So peace be upon me the day I was born, and on the day I die; and peace may be upon me on the day I shall be raised to life.

In this passage Jesus does talk about his death. He also mentions his resurrection but he might be referring to the resurrection at the end of time, rather than a special resurrection three days after his death.

Though Jesus's status and ontological controversies centring around him constitute a serious obstacle for Christian-Muslim dialogue we observe that there are considerations which mitigate the contrasts between the two religions on these issues.

The historical denouement of Christian-Muslim Relations

Though the history of Christian-Muslim relations involve numerous historical events and is still an ongoing process, I will here concentrate on two episodes, which though they took place in the distant past perpetuate in the memory and consciousness of the two faith communities and still influence the mutual perceptions of the two groups. These are namely the Crusades and the reconquest of Spain.

The Crusades

The eight Crusades spanned a long period of about 200 years from the first call to crusade by Pope Urban II at the Council of Claremont in France to the eighth Crusade under Louis of France in 1247. The immediate cause for the Pope's exhortation to Christian nations for holy war against Islam was the destruction of the Church of the Holy Sepulchre in Palestine and the obstacles raised for pilgrimages to the Holy Land by the Seljuk Turk rulers. The former Arab rulers of Palestine had been more tolerant and less obstructive to Christian pilgrims.

Palestine is holy not only to the Jews and Christians but also to Muslims basically due to being the homeland of the common patriarchs of the three faiths, and other great prophets including Prophet Isa or Jesus of Islam. Moreover Jerusalem had a special significance to Muslims as having been the city from where Prophet Mohammed had undertaken the momentous mystical journey to heaven, the *Miraj*.

The primary motivation for the Crusades was religious, namely the restoration and establishment of Christian control over places sacred to them. There were many Christians from the nations of northern Europe who participated out of genuine religious fervour, but there were many other factors involved in the genesis of this great mass movement. Some of these were political. The timing of the call to crusade was itself strategic, as in the 11th century the Muslim world was divided and the Arabs hated the Seljuk Turks, the rulers of Palestine. The fall of the Christian Byzantine Empire to Muslims at Manzhikert in 1071 had been a source of apprehension to the Christian world and they desired to close this breach in the Christian rampart safeguarding Europe from the increasingly powerful Muslims. As far as Pope Urban was concerned, the Crusade was also a strategy to re-establish the flagging supremacy of the Papacy which was being increasingly challenged by restive

Christian nations such as England, Germany and France. The Pope was hopeful that the identification of a common enemy and a united offensive against him would help to heal the schisms in the church, a strategy that ultimately did not come to fruition. As for the rulers of the Christian nations this was an opportunity to strengthen their authority by sublimating the violence in their land by directing it to an external purpose, and to send away some of the recalcitrant nobility and their forces which could have been at least a restrictive force if not an absolute threat to their sovereignty.

The economic gains from the Crusades to the Christians could not also be overlooked. Pope Urban II had indeed promised to the Christian nations at Claremont, "The possessions of the enemy will be yours, since you will make spoil of his treasures". Palestine in Biblical description was a land flowing with milk and honey. The riches of the fabulous Orient, the fabled riches of Islamic kingdoms, were no small inducement to the impoverished of the proletariat as well as the aristocracy. The landless labourers, and younger sons of the nobility who were denied fiefdoms in their own countries due to the inheritance laws prevailing then, could carve out baronies for themselves in the conquered lands.

It is strange that a faith which in its ethics places emphasis on non-violence and passive retaliation to evil, "turning the other cheek" should embark upon purposeful and deliberate conflict. Christ was also against territorial conquest. My kingdom is not of this world, he emphasised. The messianic expectations of the Jews were not fulfilled in him, and thus they did not recognise him as "the one that was to come", the Christ, anointed of God to be their liberator.

The Christian Crusaders perpetrated atrocities not only on Muslim "infidels" but also on Jews and the Eastern Christians. Indeed Sir Steven Runciman opines that the Eastern Christians suffered much more under the Crusaders than under the Caliphs, for they interfered with their religious customs.(5) To the Christians from the West the practices of the Eastern Christians were as outlandish as those of the Muslims, and the Crusade intended for the rescuing of these Syrian Christians led to their domination by the Papacy.

The Crusades were not without their beneficial aspects. The interaction between the West and the East, though confrontational, resulted in first hand knowledge of each other's cultures which had long been bogged down in fantasy and distortion. Usama , the impartial and unprejudiced Arab historian gives us some interesting vignettes of some 'Franks' who were so thoroughly orientalised that they did not eat pork at all. (6) There were other forms of cultural interaction - in architecture, music, sartorial fashions, weapons of war, emblems and heraldic terms. Religiously speaking the Islamic influence paved the way for later theological crises in Christendom. The Crusades led to new economic and social currents. The West developed a taste for luxury from the opulent Islamic world. Some of them greatly augmented their wealth and were able to give full expression to these new tastes. The Crusades also had a role in promoting democracy in Europe. Many of the nobles were forced to sell their land to their serfs for raising ransoms. On the other hand, since many of the nobles were away fighting the monarchs increased their authority unfettered by their powerful subjects.

But on the whole the interaction was hostile and traumatic. Thousands of lives were lost, though the Holy Sepulchre was ultimately not 'delivered' from the hands of the 'Saracens', though pilgrimages to the Holy Land became somewhat easier. The Papal aspiration for reunification of the Christian church was also not accomplished. Historians point out that the Crusades mark the turning point when Islam became inward looking and insular, and Muslim sciences, and cultural activities declined. Moreover as Francesco Gabrielli states the Christians still seem to see the enemy in the light of that old theological and racial hatred which later conflicts have embittered. (7) The Crusades still remain in Muslim memory and consciousness, as an unprovoked, unexpected and devastating onslaught on them by the Christian kingdoms of the West. This is revealed in Muslims characterising actions by Christian powers affecting them adversely as 'Crusade', the Gulf war, for instance.

The reconquest of Spain, the 'Reconquista'

This was an earlier episode in Christian Muslim relations, second only in significance to the Crusades, and again involved Christians and Muslims in traumatic confrontation, not in the Holy land but in

Southern Europe itself, in the Iberian Peninsula. Muslims had ruled Spain from 711 AD to almost the end of the 15th Century which saw the complete ousting of Muslims from Iberia. The reconquering of Spain by Christians, the Reconquista lasted for well nigh seven centuries. The Muslim period of Spain is now looked upon as the golden age of Spain, a meeting of the East and the West, which resulted in glorious architectural creations such as the Alhambra and the Mosque of Cordoba, the special charm and quality of Spanish music and dance, the making of delicately carved ornaments, tapestries and carpets with intricately woven patterns, processing and embossing of leather, manufacture of silk and crystal. Of great benefit to Europe was the preservation and transmission of great Greek philosophical works, especially Aristotelian philosophy, which were initially translated into Arabic and then into Latin. All areas of art and other human activities flourished, whether in music, medicine, philosophy or mathematics. Spain produced great philosophers and scientists such as al Farabi, ibn Sina (Avicenna), Ibn Rushd (Averroes) and the Jewish philosopher Maimonides.

Many of the Spanish of that time especially the Mozarabs (Christians who had lived for long under Muslim rule) considered their Muslim rulers to be more humane and benevolent (except for the Berbers who were invited by Muslim kings to assist them against Christian invasion and turned out to be a case of the medicine being worse than the disease), than their new Christian conquerors, when with the advent of the inquisition in 1480, and great rigours in religious dogma and fanaticism, the kings and the Church sought to impose religious unity by force. Spanish society of the time was very diverse, with Mudejar Muslims, Moriscoes (Muslim converts to Christianity), Jews, Mozarabs (Arabic speaking Christians), Marranos (Jewish converts to Christianity) etc. Glick states that much of the dynamism and vigour of social relations in Islamic Spain had been due to the diversity of the population which was unparalleled then in Europe.[8] The Muslim rulers had been tolerant to their Christian and Jewish subjects. Wine drinking for instance had not been frowned upon and was treated lightly, though Islamic law banned it and prescribed a punishment of 80 lashes.

As a result of the Reconquista, Spain became a society organised for war. Great financial strain was placed upon the inhabitants, both

Christian and Muslim, with the constant raids, plundering and the *'Pariahs'*, enormous amounts of money demanded by the Christian conquerors as part of a 'protection racket'. Due to the heavy expenditure incurred in wars the State came to rely on the Church to a greater extent for funds, and thus the Church became more politically involved and powerful. The Reconquista also led to the disintegration of Spain. Portugal became independent. That great adventurer Roderigo De Vivar, the infamous El Cid, established Valencia as an independent kingdom. Castile broke away from Leon.

There were some incidental benefits. There was upward social mobility for poor knights. Many freemen became nobles, and commoners had the opportunity to perform knightly duties. The society became more egalitarian as the distinctions between commoners, knights and nobles blurred. (The commoners who became knights were interestingly named *Caballieros Villanos*.) New frontier towns developed, such as Segovia and Avila. However in the ultimate analysis there were more adverse consequences than benefits from the Reconquista, and this significant event may well be considered to be the second most bitterest episode in Christian-Muslim relations, and one which vitiated such relations for a long time to come in the future. A glorious culture, the fusion of all that was best in Islamic and European civilisation was devastated, though vestiges do remain. The Reconquista marked the end of not only a glorious era of European history, but also of mutually beneficial Christian-Muslim relations.

Conclusion

As I have mentioned at the outset, there is much potential for harmonious relations between Islam and Christianity. The Qur'an positively enjoins it. (Sura 5:85) Christianity is a religion which emphasises non-violence and loving and sympathetic relationships. Though there are significant doctrinal dissimilarities there is also much common ground between these faiths. But the history of violent confrontations such as the Crusades and the Reconquista continue to colour mutual perspectives, foment prejudice and vitiate such relations. Political intrigues in many parts of the world continue to embitter what could easily become an ideal for interaction between two major faiths. However it is heartening to note that religious leaders of both communities are emphasising nowadays the need for greater tolerance, understanding, and dialogue rather than polemics and denigration of each other's faith. Most major Christian churches have dialogue wings and are keenly trying enter into dialogue with Muslims and other faiths, and in some instances have even made attempts to hold united worship. Many recognise Islam as a valuable ally against rising materialism and secularism, and moral and ethical decline in the world. Muslim initiatives are also not lacking. (for instance the work of the Islam and Modern Age Society founded by the late Dr. Abid Hussayn in India in 1978, and the Indian Institute for Islamic Studies.[9] Both religions have much to learn from each other. Christian emphasis on love, and peaceful relationships and Muslim commitment, religious fervour and discipline can greatly contribute to each other's religious and social life. Unfortunately fundamentalism is on the increase in many regions of the world, due mainly to issues related to culture, power, and financial privileges, rather than of purely religious factors. Culture is no doubt important, but universal religions such as Islam and Christianity should be able to transcend narrow cultural divides and parochialism. In the subsequent chapters we will look into a region where Christianity and Islam are powerful religious and social entities, namely, Sarawak in East Malaysia.

References

1. See Acts Chapter 15.
2. see Sheikh, M. S., (1982), *Islamic Philosophy*, The Octagon Press: London, p. 63.
3. See John 14:7, and 14:10.
4. Hick, J. (Edr), (1977)*The Myth of God Incarnate*, SCM Press: London.

5. Runciman, S., (1964), "The Crusades, a Moral Failure", in Brundage, J. A., *The Crusades, Motives and Achievements*, D.C. Heath and Co.: Lexington, pp. 75-81, p. 78.

6. Quoted in Gabrielli, Francesco (1969)*Arab Historians of the Crusades*, (Costello, E.J., Tr.), Routledge and Kegan Paul: London, p. 79.

7. Ibid, (Introduction) p. xi.

8. Glick, T. F., (1979)*Islamic and Christian Spain in the Early Middle Ages*, Princeton University Press: Princeton, p. 165.

9. See Troll, C. W. (1979), "Christian-Muslim Relations in India", *Islamo Christiana*, No. 5, pp. 119 to 145.

3 The Malay-Muslim equation

The word *Malay* (Melayu) connotes a race rather than a religious group. The anthropologist Kroeber describes the racial characteristics of the Malay thus:

> Straight hair, slight body hairs, broad head, medium width of nose, brown skin colour, below average stature [1].

To this we can perhaps add a genial and gentle manner, but one which hides passion and courage when aroused. The Malays and the Bhumiputra belong to the wider category known as the Mongoloids, which includes the Chinese, the Mongols of Central Asia and the American Indian. It is interesting to note that this definition will cover most of the indigenous tribes of Sarawak and Sabah. The indigenous inhabitants of Malaya, collectively known as Bhumiputra (sons of the soil, from the Sanskrit roots Bhumi = earth, and Putra= son) are not racially much different from the Malays. As a matter of fact the anthropological and scientific usage of the term *Malay* will cover the original inhabitants of the entire Malay archipelago such as the Filipinos and the Indonesians, in addition to the Malaysians. But the legal definition of a Malay is much more restrictive. According to the Malaysian constitution a Malay is a person professing the Muslim religion, habitually speaks Malay and conforms to Malay custom. (Article 160) There are also some stipulations as to his/her year of birth and parentage. It is evident from this definition that adherence to Islam is an important factor in Malaynness along with language and etiquette and customs. The language and customs factor however cannot always be insisted upon, for instance as S. Husin Ali points out,[2] a Malay/Muslim educated in an English public school may speak only English, and moreover may be so westernised that he does not conform to Malay etiquette and customs in his day-to-day life style, but he will not however be prevented from considering himself as a Malay and is eligible for the special privileges of a Malay/Bhumiputra

It is significant that this definition does not stipulate any racial characteristics as a criterion for Malay status. As a matter of fact two of the top-most contemporary UMNO (United Malay National Organisation)leaders, Prime Minister Mahathir Mohammed and Deputy Prime Minister Anwar Ibrahim are of Indian Muslim origins. Husin Ali points out that descendants of Pakistanis, Indian Muslims and Arabs have been regarded as Malays and granted Malay privileges. Thus, Islam seems to be the most important factor of Malay identity. It is to be noted that in Sarawak the Melanaus, the majority of whom are Muslims, are the perennial allies of the Malays in the region and this alliance dominates the political scene there. The Ibans, the largest ethnic group are largely Christian, and has traditionally considered the Malays as their enemies.[3] This must be, though not overtly, at least at a subconscious and incipient level, an important factor in Christian-Muslim relations in Sarawak, and in the recent resurgence of Dayak consciousness and mobilisation in politics. If religion is such an important criterion in the Malay identity why are Muslims from Indian, Chinese etc. ethnic origins not accorded the same status as the Malays, and other non-Malays when they embrace Islam? Granting them such privileges would be a very strong impetus for Muslim proselytisation. The Bapa Malaysia (Father of the Nation - Tunku Abdul Rahman) strongly advocated this step. He urged that all Malaysians, irrespective of ethnicity or race be considered as Malays when they embrace Islam.

It is not that the Tunku was against special privileges for the Malays. He felt that the non-Bhumiputras who are born and brought up here are imbued with the nation's ethos and traditions, and only the religious factor is lacking to fulfil the criteria for Malaynness. It is clear that the Tunku considered Islam as an intrinsic and the most important factor of Malay identity.

The Malays argue strongly that they are the original and therefore the true inhabitants of the land. The nation rightly belongs to them. There seem to be two factors in the genesis of this emotion, factors which are to some extent mutually contradictory. On the one hand their concept of ownership of the country is perhaps a reaction to the long period of foreign occupation and dominance, when they were a subordinate class in their own land and moreover came to be economically, educationally and even geographically in the backwaters of the nation. On the other hand, the British tried to legitimise their hegemony through patronising the Malay royalty who symbolised both the Malayness of the country and their dominant status in the nation. Both these factors helped to augment Malay consciousness. The Malays also feel that the Chinese and Indian presence in the region is not at their invitation, but rather a British imposition on them, an importation from abroad which gradually supplanted the Malay masses demographically and economically.(4) Even today many Malays speak of a Chinese Bangsa, (nation) and an Indian Bangsa and call them Orang Asing (foreign people). (5) To some extent, they consider the Chinese and Indian an unwelcome intrusion into their land, exploiting its resources which are rightfully theirs. The apprehension that they will become second class citizens in their own nation was very real to the Malays. Though the Malay archipelago had been in the distant past a bastion of Hindu-Buddhist religion and culture, vestiges of which are quite tangible in the arts and folk Islamic praxis, for most of the present generation and especially for the young modernists who argue for a pure form of Islam in the Wahabi model, it was not only a matter of racial but also of religious disparities, as most of the Chinese and Indians are followers of Far- Eastern faiths and the Hindu religion. Thus it was not only their Malay ethnicity but also the religion of Islam which set the Malays apart and gave them a distinct identity. Thus the Malay/Muslim equation became vital to the UMNO, ABIM, PAS(6) and others clamouring for Malay supremacy in the body politic. (It is to be remembered that Dr. Mahathir, the present Prime Minister, had at one time been an advocate of one-party rule and had been expelled from the UMNO for this reason). Thus matters such as the refining of Islam, divesting of Hindu/Buddhist/animistic practices, and the suppression of "deviant" forms of Islam such as Qudiyanism became important. The Hindu-animistic associations and deviant forms or false teachings could not only dilute the doctrinal basis of orthodox Islam but also split the Malay community as indeed it already has with the Kuam Muda and Kuam Tuan factions and the emergence of puritanical political parties such as PAS, and Dar al Arquam. (7) The promotion and dominance of Islam vis- a-vis Hinduism, Christianity etc. thus become important to sustain Malay ascendancy. It is no wonder then that in Sarawak where Christians form the largest group the administration still is led by the Malay/Melanau Muslim group, there is a preponderance of Muslims in the bureaucracy, and that alleged discrimination against even Bhumiputra Christians as in the case of Charles Soang of the Dewan Bahasa dan Pustaka organisation, takes place.

Islam is a religion which in comparison to many others, perhaps with the exception of Judaism, invites the largest proportion of adherents to a very strong commitment to the faith and its practice. Its very structure with five daily prayers, month-long fasting, obligatory alms-giving and a cherished ambition to perform the Hajj at least once in a lifetime, besides the suzerainty of Islamic law over the whole of life, commands much commitment and zeal in maintaining the faith. In many ways it is much closer to Judaism than to Christianity, especially in its emphasis on ritual, the *Ibadah*, and the significance attached to *Sharia*, Islamic religious law. Witnessing the faith and martyrdom, linked by the related Arabic terms Shahada and *Shahid* are highly extolled, and testify to the stress on loyalty to the faith. Apostasy is frowned upon and is theoretically punishable by death. It is a keen proselytising faith and there is a burning desire in genuine Muslims to warn non-believers about impending judgement and punishment. Fawcett speaking about the Muslims of Central Malabar in India remarks on the tenacity of new converts to the faith, whom he states become as zealous of Islam as those who are born in the faith in families which have been Muslim for centuries, in spite of the fact that some of these converts joined Islam under duress.(8) In the Mappila rebellion of 1921 in India the British often saw Muslim soldiers and policemen joining their co-religionists--loyalty to the faith over-riding loyalty to their pay masters and political overlords. (9) Islam seems to have that special chemistry which promotes commitment, zeal and community solidarity. As Hussin Muttalib states, Islam is ingrained in the Malay psyche. (10) Islam is part and parcel of the Malay *weltanschaung*, their language, oral traditions etc. The British added strength to the Islamic consciousness of the Malays by utilising the Sultans, who are also head the Islamic faith in their dominions, and Islamic law in combination with *adat* or Malay auxiliary law and English Common Law to smoothen the administration of their Malay colonial possessions. By acknowledging the supremacy of Islam the British paved the way for the predominance of Islam in post-Merdeka Malaysia.

Regan Daniel has done some research into the religiosity of the Malays and their commitment to external practices of religion. His analysis presented in his book *Secular City - The Religious Orientations of Intellectuals in Malaysia,* reveals 25% of the Malays as deeply religious and 72% as moderately religious as against 3% and 8% respectively in these categories among the non-Malays. Similarly while 77% of the Malays are committed to external religious practices only 7% are so committed among the non-Malays. (11) It is significant that the strong commitment these figures reveal are prevalent among the intelligentsia, and reiterates that the Islamic revival in Malaysia is strongest among the urban educated and not in the rural kampong folk, quite the reverse of what would normally be expected.

Conversion of a Malay to non-Islamic faiths is rare but has happened in the past. In such cases they lose their Malay status. In India, the scheduled castes/tribes who are considered to be part of Hindu religion, (though theoretically the *avarnas* or outcastes do not belong to the Hindu fold, and the tribals have their distinctive gods and religious practices) do not lose their special status and privileges when they convert to other faiths such as Islam, Christianity or Buddhism. Such conversions do take place and occasionally in large numbers. The Malay however does not lose constitutional privileges when he/she becomes so anglicised/westernised that he/she loses touch with his/her mother tongue and the Malay customs. Thus Islam seems to be more significant as a factor in Malayness than cultural aspects such as language and customs. Groups who are racially Malay in an anthropological and scientific sense such as the Javanese, Achenese, and Benjarese are not eligible for the constitutional privileges, while Malays of mixed descent, when one parent is Pakistani/ Indian/ Arab and are Muslim do obtain these advantages. Therefore strictly speaking neither race nor language nor culture is the paramount factor in Malayness but rather Islam mixed with some amount of Malay blood. On the other hand Indian and Chinese Muslims and converts to Islam from Hindu and Far Eastern religions do not attain Bhumiputra status though they may have been born and brought up in Malaysia and their families resident there for decades.

The effect of extremist and fundamentalist political organisations such as the PAS, Dar al Arquam, and Jamat- i- Tablighi [12] would only serve to highlight the Islamic factor of Malay identity. That the colonial masters and the West, viewed as corrupting the Islamic world and eroding Islamic values, are rightly or wrongly associated with the Christian faith does not augur well for good Christian-Muslim relations in Malaysia. Dr. Muzzafar Chandra has pointed out that the Malay/Muslim equation would not be a problem but for the overall communal environment of the nation.[13]   In India, a country which started out on the basis of the equality of all religions, of late the Hindu character of national identity is more and more forcibly stressed by prominent political groups such as the BJP, who takes the view that to be an Indian is to be a Hindu. The coalescing of national identity with one particular religion has led to much disruption there. Incidents such as that of the destruction of the Babri mosque in Ayodhya and consequent widespread communal riots and bomb explosions in Bombay have adversely affected inter-religious harmony. It is evident that religious harmony cannot be established in India on the basis of Hindutva or Hinduness, the slogan of the BJP. It should be remembered that unlike Muslims in Malaysia, in India the Hindus are in the vast majority. However the populace seems to be at present disillusioned with the BJP and their sloganeering of *Hindutva* and appeal to the Hinduness of the nation. They have lost the recent state elections in Uttar Pradesh, their stronghold. The Indian experience is relevant to what is happening in Malaysia. The UMNO administration and the PAS seem to be engaging in an Islamisation game, which may trigger off a reaction of religious and cultural revivalism among the non-Muslims. There are organisations such as Aliran, the Ministry of National Unity, the Malaysian Consultative Council of Buddhism, Christianity, Hinduism and Sikhism (MCCBHS), whose objective is to promote inter-communal harmony, but many seem to be skeptical of their achievements. Rev. Aries, the principal of the Kuching Theological College whom I met told me frankly that in view of continuing discrimination and preferential treatment of Malay/Muslim, the rapid Islamicisation of the nation and the call for an Islamic State, the situation of national integration/harmony seems to be deteriorating rather than ameliorating. The PAS and other fundamentalist organisations seem to have very little contact with Christian and other non-Muslim communities. (14) They seem to have little interest in entering into dialogue with these faiths. They criticise the Mahathir administration as un-Islamic. The Dar al Arqam especially has recently been scathing in their allegations against the government of being un-Islamic. Such allegations push the government into taking steps to outflank the fundamentalist parties by intensifying its Islamisation programme, whether it be symbolic institutions such as an Islamic bank or more financial support for Islamic institutions, or the appointment of a body to study how Islamic principles could form the basis of national development programmes. The Malaysian Federal and state administration seem to be genuinely under the apprehension that they will be losing their popular base to the fundamentalists, so great is the identification between political power and Islam. This Islamicisation race between the Muslim parties and the government is truly frightening for the non-Malays and Christians etc., but the internal security Act and the Sensitive Issues Amendments have effectively silenced public voicing of their opposition to the biassed actions of the government. Such suppression is not only undemocratic but in the long run counter productive as far as inter-religious and inter-ethnic relations are concerned.

There is a possibility that the new measures regarding language, culture etc., especially in the educational field, will in the long run tend to eliminate the heterogeneity of the Malaysian populace. The promotion of Bahasa Malaysia in schools is an instance to the point. The Chinese have been much disturbed by the appointment of non-Chinese speaking Headmasters in Chinese schools. Government assurances not withstanding, the tendency seems to be the gradual suppression of what are perceived to be alien languages -- Chinese, Tamil etc. The predominance of the Bahasa in the educational field (as medium of instruction), in officialdom (as the language of government) and in public affairs (road signs, official ceremonies etc.) can gradually lead to the eclipse and even ultimate extinction of the non- Malay languages. Language is an important factor in the formation of culture and in due course the Malayisation process would extend to factors such as dress, etiquette and other aspects of life style. This can be compared to the westernisation of Eastern regions under colonial regimes. With the decline of cultural heterogeneity the raison d'etre for Malay political parties such as the UMNO would disappear. In such a situation the Malay-Muslim equation would take on a new importance and significance. Thus Islam would become the greater symbol of national identity than Malayness. The call for Islamicisation would intensify, and ultimately Malaysia would be declared an Islamic state and the jurisdiction of the Sharia extended to all citizens and not just the Muslims as at present. This is not an improbable scenario for the not too distant future. Mohammed Tawfeek Sahran, Chief Executive Secretary of BINA, the Muslim Evangelical organisation whom I met at Kuching is of the opinion that Islamicisation will be beneficial to all, not the Muslims alone. The Islamic state will be fair to them. They will be looked upon as protected citizens (*dhimmi*). He pointed out, as didUstad Kipli whom I met at the Makamah Sharia (Islamic court), that the present system was unfair to Muslims. The Shariah with its stringent rules and severe punishments is applicable only to them. Ustad Kipli pointed out that if for instance a Muslim and a non-Muslim were apprehended in a state of *Khalwat* (the offence committed according to Islamic Law when a male and a female who are not within the prohibited categories of kinship for marriage are in close proximity in isolation) only the Muslim would be punished. Of course the application of the Sharia on the Muslims is of their own choice, not an imposition on them by non-Muslims.

It is true that Islamic law envisages freedom of religion and fairness to non-Muslims. The concept of Dhimmi (protected citizens) applies to them. This signifies that in the Islamic state the religious minorities will be given special protection against hostile members of the majority community. What the safeguards are is not clear. Is it just physical protection, or does this protection extend to discrimination in avenues for employment, commerce and other economic activity, also the safety of their places of worship and all other contexts where hostile actions are possible? Islamic law envisages a special tax, the Jizyah, from non- Muslims, probably to defray the expenses incurred in giving them special protection. The Prophet did have a place in the first Islamic State, Yathrib (Madeenat-al-Nabi) for Jews and Christians. Under the constitution he drew up they had perfect freedom of worship, ownership of property, employment, in fact all fundamental rights. However in most discussions about the nature of the Islamic state by theorists it is stated that the position of head state is the prerogative of Muslims only. In Malaysia the Head of State is a Sultan and therefore a Muslim. But there is no proviso excluding non- Muslims from the office of the Chief executive, the Prime Minister or other members of the cabinet. In a recent interview in British television (Channel 4) the Malaysian Minister for Finance, Anwar Ibrahim stated that the office of the Prime Minister will reflect the majority status of the Malay/ Muslim community Is there any possibility, he asked of an Indian ever becoming the Prime Minister of Britain, or a black the President of the United States, though there are substantial minorities of Indians in the U.K, and blacks in the U.S.A.? The implication seems to be that there is an unwritten proviso excluding the non Malay/Muslim from the highest office, though technically this is possible. Sabah almost had a Christian Chief Minister, Donald Stephens, but he converted to Islam under pressure from the ruling Muslim elite. But the fact remains that the support of the Federal Government would ensure that a Muslim would head administrations of even the states in Borneo where numerically the Muslims are not in a majority. It stands to reason that if Sarawak had not joined the Malaysian Federation the different demographic patterns of the state would have more effectively come into play and instead of a Malay/Melanau leadership a Dayak-led administration would have been in place in the region, in which case the effective prominence of the Muslims in the bureaucracy and other spheres would not have taken place. As it stands the special religious and racial patterns of Sarawak have not been allowed to have their impact on the corporate life of the State.

Racially speaking the Malays and the indigenous groups of Sarawak are not vastly different. Malay distinctiveness would therefore be dependent on language, religion and customs. Religion is an important factor in the determination of culture and values. Thus the association of Islam with the Malay/Melanau would become even more crucial to maintain their distinctiveness in Sarawak. It also constitutes an important element in their affinity to the peninsular Malay society and the Federal UMNO administration. Angkatan Nahadathul Islam Bersatu (BINA) has its origins in the evangelistic organisation PERKIM founded in the Peninsula, the Tunku, Bapa Malaysia, having been one of the patrons of this mission-oriented Islamic organisation. Abdul Taib Mohammed, the Chief Minister of Sarawak is one of the founders of BINA.[16] The objectives of BINA clearly indicate the minority status of Islam in the state and calls itself a frontline Islamic organisation working for the enhancement of Dawah (Islamic revival) . [17] It states that the fact that the Chief Minister is a founding member enhances and reinforces the relationship between various religious agencies (probably of the peninsula) and BINA, and that although Muslims are a minority and the status of Islam is yet to be as Sarawak's religion, the position of Islam and Muslims is indeed a force to reckon with. [18] Though the proselytising thrust of BINA is mainly at the indigenous interior tribal people, Haji Tawfeek did mention to me of the conversion of a Samoan Christian to Islam under the auspices of the BINA. He mentioned that the motivation for the Samoan's conversion was his dissatisfaction with his church's inability to satisfy his curiosity and questions regarding God and the world, thereby implying some deficiency in the Christian church and the superiority of Islam which is able to clarify and settle human religious aspirations and their cosmological questions.

Chandra Muzzafar advocates that the administrations should

emphasise the positive aspects of Islam instead of trying to outmanoeuvre the fundamentalists in the purist game. [19] In a way if the Islamic rather than the ethnic identity is emphasised, the egalitarianism, justice and compassion of Islam would ensure fairness to all than a narrow Malay ethnocentricity. Dr. Hussin Muttalib in his *Islam and Ethnicity in Malay Politics* has provided a long list contrasting values in the Malay/Islam identity question, stressing more the egalitarian and universalistic values of Islam. [20] However how concepts such as Shariah replacing *Adat* and the holistic nature of Islamic law replacing a more secular vision of separation of religion and politics as advocated by the Tunku can be beneficial to inter- religious harmony is not clear. There are many positive points about Dr. Muttalib's juxtaposition of ethnicity and Islamicity such as protection and justice for all instead of Bhumiputra rights, Malaysia belongs to all citizens, and *Hidup Keadilan* instead of *Hidup Melayu* (long live the Malays). Juosh Hamid states that the pre-Independance Alliance party considered that the function of Islam as the official religon was for ceremonial purposes only. [21] However, Islam seems to have come a long way from this position in its association with the state. It is even more than the ties between the Church of England and the state in 'Britain. There the link is rather tenuous and seems to be mainly confined to what the Alliance Party viewed as the original role of Islam as the State religion in Malaysia--i.e. confined to ceremonial purposes. The very fact that as prominent a champion of Islamic revival as Anwar Ibrahim, leader of the ABIM joined the UMNO testifies to its Islamic credentials and the tendency for the coalescing of ethnic and religious identity of the Malay people. The main opposition to the Government in power--a coalition of Malay UMNO, Indian MIC and Chinese MCA--is Islamic fundamentalist revivalist PAS, not the Chinese or the Indians. The struggle has now passed from the ethnic to the religious dimension of Malayness. As Negata points out the struggle now is to present oneself as the better Muslim [22]

In Sarawak the Malay/Muslim had fluctuating fortunes. Under the Brooke regime the Malays had been favoured and was the dominant group in the civil service. But the Brooks had also encouraged and assisted the immigration of the Chinese, and they eventually dominated the non agricultural sectors of the economy and education. Moreover they mainly settled in the urban areas which are the centres of political power. The main contenders against the Malays in politics during the British Raj (1946-1963) were the Chinese, not the Dayaks and other indigenous groups. The colonial policy of open recruitment also meant that the Malays no longer dominated the Civil Service.

During the early days of the Post-Merdeka period, the Federal and the Sarawak leadership were in continual conflict for instance on the question of language. The Malays were particularly incensed that the national language, the Malay based Bahasa Malaysia, was not accepted by Sarawak as one of the official languages. (They did accept the Bahasa as the national language, but opted to retain English as the official language till the state legislature enacted legislation switching over to Bahasa Malaysia as the national language). Prime Minister Tunku Abdul Rahman stated that "the language is the soul of the nation". (23) The Tunku genuinely desired national unity and a unified culture, of which language is one of the principal elements, but not under the banner of Islam, though he did feel Islam to be the criterion for Malayness, overriding considerations of ethnicity, customs etc.

However, after the 1970 state elections the Abdu Rahman Yakub administration in a forceful and skilful way was gradually able to assert the influence of federal policies, mainly based on the Malay/Muslim ideology, in Sarawak, particularly those regarding education and religion. The non- Malay/non- Muslim sections of the population, though much disturbed, could not effectively voice their criticism due to the existence of the ISA and other regulations restricting expression of dissent. This was similar to what was happening in the Peninsula, but in the light of the minority situation of the Malay/Muslims groups in Sarawak this state of affairs was indeed extraordinary for a democracy. Yakub however, after his dethronement from power and his controversies with his successor Mohammed Taib, his own nephew, did ally with the Dayaks, probably not due to an ideological change but rather as a political stratagem against his rival, the present Chief Minister.

The cause of national integration and inter-ethnic/inter-religious harmony could have been better achieved if the "positive discrimination", the special privileges and concessions in employment, education etc. had been awarded on the basis of economic/employment status and educational achievements and such criteria on an individual basis rather than on the basis of ethnicity. The blanket eligibility conferred now on the Malay/ Muslim and Bhumiputra gives rise to many anomalies. Dr. Tan Chee Beng criticises the assumption that all Chinese are richer than the Malays. (24) He states that the class differences within each ethnic group has been ignored. Frustration is generated when the poor non-Malay/non-Bhumiputra sees many rich Malays availing of privileges which they are denied in spite of their poverty. The dynamics of social mobility due to these concessions are ignored. In India, there is a decennial review of these privileges. In Malaysia, probably because the issue is so politicised there is no such process, and the privileges are granted permanently to the Malay/Bhumiputra. Beng is right in saying that this aggravates the polarisation, especially when it is the middle class and the upper classes among the Malay/Bhumiputra who are benefiting from these concessions.(25) The preponderance of the Malay/Muslim in the bureaucratic system, currently 4/5 of its strength, leads to an informal networking, nepotism and a superiority consciousness among them of being the ruling race/religious group. This leads to dissatisfaction and a persecution complex among Christians and other minorities. The situation in the Peninsula is affecting Sarawak and Sabah where the Christians/Dayaks are quite numerically strong, but do not seem to possess their fair share of the political/administrative power.

It is certain that the ethnic and religious minorities of Malaysia acceded to the special status and privileges of the Malay/ Muslim not in virtue of their numerical superiority which is marginal, nor their avowed status as the original inhabitants of the land, but in view of their economic and educational backwardness. However the Malay/Muslims have politicised the issue out of recognition and claim their special status as a natural prerogative, and aver that the Chinese/Indian minorities are alien groups (*Orang Asing*) who are to be tolerated rather than accepted as citizens of Malaysia entitled equally to all the rights and prerogatives which nationality confers on them. The increasing coalescing of Islam with national identity would make Christians, Hindus and other minority religious groups also highly suspect, with their right to be citizens and their loyalty to the nation questioned. Such attitudes can lead to explosive situations such as currently taking place in Sri Lanka, where a parallel to the Malay/non-Malay polarisation exists between the Singhalese/Tamil groups. It is to be remembered that unlike the Chinese/ Buddhist/ Indian/ Hindu/ Sikh/ Christian groups of Malaysia the Tamils of Sri Lanka have inhabited the island nation for more than 600 years, but intolerance, mutual suspicion and discrimination have arisen between them and the Singhalese. The leaders of Malaysia and the Government in power and the opposition have to think seriously and set in motion effective strategies to prevent such a situation, rather than outmanoeuvering each other in the Islamicisation of the body politic and the national ethos. Bodies such as the National Unity Board have not achieved much. In Sarawak, where on the religious front the communities are more or less evenly balanced this would have been much easier to achieve had the Federal Government allowed a consensus and rapport to develop between the various religious communities, without imposing the same policies, attitudes and structure which has to some extent vitiated inter-religious relations in West Malaysia.

Notes

6. UMNO= United Malay National Organisation
ABIM= Angkatan Belia Islam Malaysia (Islamic Youth Movement of Malaysia).
PAS= Partai Islam se Malaysia (Islamic Party of Malaysia)
7. Dar al Arqam= House (Land) of Arqam, an Islamic revivalist organisation (Arqam was a friend of Prophet Mohammed).
12. Jamat-i- Tabligh (lit.) Association for Service to God, an Islamic revivalist organisation of Indian Muslim origins.

References

1. Kroeber, A.L. (1967), *Anthropology*, Oxford and I.B.H. Publishing

Co : New Delhi, p. 131.

2. Ali, S. Husin (1981), *The Malays, their Problems and Future*, Heinemann Asia: Kuala Lumpur, p. 3.

3. Ibid, p. 5.

4. Ibid, p. 7.

5. Soong, Kua Kia,(Edr) (1990), *Malaysian Cultural Policy and Democracy*, The Resources and Research Centre : Kuala Lumpur, p. 16.

8. Fawcett, F. (October 1897), "The Moplahs of Malabar", *The Imperial and Asiatic Quarterly Review*, pp. 288-299, p. 289.

9. Ibid.

10. Muttalib, Hussin (1990), *Islam and Ethnicity in Malay Politics*, Oxford University Press: Singapore, p. 31.

11. Regan, Daniel (1977) "Secular City- The Religious Orientations of Intellectuals in Malaysia", in Lent, John A., (Edr), *Cultural Pluralism in Malaysia*, North Illinois University Centre for South East Asian Studies; Illinois, pp. 43-56, p. 48.

13. Muzaffar, Chandra (1987), *Islamic Resurgence in Malaysia*, Penerbit Fajar Bakti Sadan BHD: Petaling Jeya, p. 20.

14. Ibid, p. 10.

15. Angkatan Nahadathul Islam Bersatu (United Islamic Renaissance Movement) (1993), *BINA, a Brief Introduction*, BINA: Kuching, p. 3.

16. Ibid.

17. Ibid.

18. Ibid.

19. Khoon, Tan Chee (1984), in *Contemporary Issues in Malay religions*, MCCBHS : Pelanduk Publications: Petaling Jeya, p. 21.

20. Muttalib, H., op. cit., p. 159.

21. Jusoh, Hamid (1991), *The Position of Islamic Law in the Malaysian Constitution*, Dewan Bahasa dan Pustaka Kementerian Pendidikan Malaysia: Kuala Lumpur, p. 22.

22. Negata, Judith (1987), "Indices of the Islamic Resurgence in Malaysia, The Medium and the Message", in Antoun and Hegland (Edrs.), *Religious Resurgence*, Syracuse University Press, 1987: New York, pp. 108-126, p. 114.

23. Soong, op. cit., p.226.

24. in Khoon, Tan Chee (1985), *Malaysia Today*, Pelanduk Publications: Petaling Jeya, p. 24.

4 *Dawah*, the Islamic call

The Islamic resurgence in the world, which has manifested itself in many parts of the Muslim world since the 1970s was highlighted by the overthrow of the Shah in Iran and the emergence of Khomeini as the symbol of radical fundamentalist Islam and the great champion and ideologue of *Dar al Islam* (Land of Islam). The phenomenon has not passed Malaysia by. The reasons for this resurgence are manifold. The occupation of most of the Islamic world by European powers in the 19th and early 20th centuries, and the consequent cultural colonialism were perceived not only as political humiliation of Islam but also as eroding Islamic traditions and values, which needed to be restored. Thus part of this revival was to counter the threat that Western culture and in some cases, as in India and South East Asia, Western Christian Missions posed for Islam. Another factor was that Islamic countries experienced a phase of modernisation and emulation of the west under regimes led mostly by western-educated elites, who were favourably disposed to European powers, at the expense of their natural resources such as Petroleum, and built up social institutions and educational systems in the Western model. It was now time for the Islamic identity, ways of life and values to reassert itself. Debate about western style modernism vs. Islam is not simply at the theoretical or ideological level. It is on the other hand predominantly political and can mobilise the force of arms and large numbers of committed and courageous *Mujahiddin* (warriors) to its cause. Iran, Egypt, Algeria, Morocco etc. are actually witnessing the reassertion of Islam in a very aggressive and militant manner. In his discussion of the concept of the Islamic state the Ayatollah does exhort Islamic nations to rise up and establish *Dar al Islam*. (1) The call is for a Jihad (Holy War) against non - Islamic regimes and the norms, values, culture etc. instituted by them. The Islamic nations where as of yet Islamic law is not supreme is thus *Dar al Harb* (land of war). The underlying rationale and justification for Islamicisation of the state is that Islam is a panacea for all evil, corruption, moral decline and the overall degeneration of society based on Western values. The cessation of unIslamic activities such as night clubs, discos, and even the cinema, and the promotion of morally correct activities such as Qur'an reading, devotions, Islamic discussions and seminars, and wearing the correct Islamic dress are advocated. The wholesale implementation of the *Shariah* will bring to an end all the evil and corruption which derive from a deviation from Islam. The ideology has the appeal of being simple, decisive and complete. The dichotomy between Islam and the absence of Islam is positive and clear cut. There are no shades of grey.

I have already mentioned in the last chapter the strong commitment and zeal that Islam engenders in comparison to most other religions, except perhaps Judaism. The idea of the Islamic state, where Islam/*Shariah* is supreme is one which appeals strongly to the religious sentiments of Muslims. The PAS, ABIM and other Islamic parties of Malaysia often criticise the UMNO of being un-Islamic and of emphasising ethnicity (*asabiyya*) above Islam. It is critical of the UMNO leaders who wish Islam to be progressive i.e. in a Western sense. It accuses that their strategies for development disregard Islam and succumb entirely to Western ideology. Mahathir counters in two ways. One by turning to a "Look East" policy emulating Japan/Korea rather than the West. However this is only disguising the problem, according to the fundamentalists, substituting a Far-Eastern "European" model for a Western European model. Secondly in his *The Challenge* Mahathir stresses the need to guard and defend the Islamic way of life and values by resorting to and becoming skilled in the economic, and more importantly, the technological and defence sectors of activity, for which he recognises the Western model as not only supreme but tacitly accepted by the whole world as such. (2) Therefore he attempts to mitigate the contrasts between the Islamic and the Western, at least in the fields of Science and Technology, since for the the Muslim fundamentalist/zealot anything Western is corrupt and anti-Islamic, not only in the cultural but even in the scientific spheres of human activity. Mahathir argues that what is now perceived as Western had its origins in the Muslim world be it philosophy, science or technology. To some extent he is correct. Some of the seminal concepts and procedures in science as well as arts and philosophy is Middle- Eastern in origin. But its full and modern development is by the West, though many eastern nations are now contributing to innovations and applications which are fast outstripping the West. Therefore how far the Islamic parties will accept Mahathir's contention is uncertain. The fact is that, as Ali Merad points out, some of the political objectives of the Islamic resurgence are beyond the abilities and the natural domain of religion (3) But the ideologues of the Islamic state and revival want a wholesale Islamicisation. The concept, as I have stated earlier, has a strong appeal to Muslim religious sentiments. In the last chapter I have argued that in Malaysia Islam is fast outstripping ethnicity or race as the essential element of Malayness.(4) Thus the exhortations and aspirations of PAS, Dar al Arquam etc. strike a sympathetic chord in Malay/Muslim minds. The UMNO administration is aware of this and seems with symbolic gestures such as the Islamic Bank, Islamic University, Islamic insurance, Qur'an reading competitions etc. to counter the threat from the radical Islamic parties, while at the same time as Sundaram and Cheek state being wary of the Ulama (5). Mahathir and Anwar are no doubt in a personal sense committed to Islam but they are not fully convinced that the wholesale implementation of the *Shariah* is practicable and will not leave Malaysia floundering behind other developing nations in the economic and technological fields. The Bapa Malaysia and moderates such as Chandra Muzzafar are apprehensive of the effect that Islamicisation of the state will have on such a pluralistic society as Malaysia. Sundaram and Cheek opine that most non-Muslim citizens of Malaysia feel threatened and helpless at the increasing, powerful and assertive advocacy of Islam by the radical parties. (6)

The *Shariah* does have many positive points to it. Its egalitarianism within the Islamic Umma, its moral rectitude and discipline, its emphasis on solidarity and helping the weak, are virtues which most nations extol and wish to implement. The weakness of the *Shariah* lies in its inadaptability to modern needs and circumstances. It took its final shape in the 10th century A.D. and since then there is a ban on modification dependant on the cessation of *idjma*(consensus), *ijtihad* (personal interpretation) *qiyas* (analogy) and other processes associated with its formulation. Its provisions for penal law and ban on interest and such laws need to be modified in the light of the changing social, ideological and technological circumstances. But the orthodox insists it is for all time. Modern Muslim thinkers such as Abdu and Rida of Egypt, and Shariati of Iran are more flexible, speaking of a purely religious aspect of the *Shariah* (Ibadat) which is immutable and a social or more secular aspect(Muammalat) in which modifications conformable to the needs and circumstance of the age are possible. Such flexibility is needed if Islamic law is to be compatible with the exigencies of modern life. The world has turned into a global village and Islamic nations cannot function in isolation from the rest of the world.

The experience in Iran, Pakistan etc. has had a strong impact on Malaysia and other parts of the Islamic world. However, considerable ingenuity has been needed in Pakistan, for instance in resolving the financial implications of the *Shariah*, and they have still not surmounted the problems, fresh hurdles are constantly cropping up on the issue of banking, interest etc. Schacht points out that even in medieval times, the ban on *riba* (usury) had been circumvented by the use of collateral such as land, which could be tilled and the produce taken by the lender, this being a form of recompense for the money lent. (7) Many scholars are of the opinion that it was against extortionate interest and consequent victimisation of the borrower, not against some legitimate forms of remuneration for the lender, that the Qur'an and the Prophet instituted the law on interest. But in later times and even today the law became very rigid, and the letter rather than the spirit of the *Shariah* prevailed.

The other significant factor in the world-wide resurgence of Islam and the sometimes militant and aggressive form it assumes is the

54

Palestinian issue. The plight of the Palestinians and the confrontation of Israel with the Arab states have shown Muslims how vulnerable they are, and how European nations could control and manipulate the course of events in the Middle East. The future of Muslim states as in the colonial times seem to rest in Western hands--a kind of neocolonialism of which the USA is seen as the chief protagonist. The Palestinian issue has created much hostility against not only Israel but also against America and other Western nations involved in what Muslims term the Zionist cause. Though many Muslims who are not directly affected by the Israeli-Arab confrontation may not overtly express their displeasure and rancour against the West, in their heart of hearts Muslims in India, Malaysia etc. feel sympathy for their Palestinian co-religionists and resentment against the West which supports Israel. The recent thaw in Arab-Israeli relations will go some way to ameliorating these attitudes, but the significance of the Palestinian issue in the genesis of the anti-western rhetoric and actions of Islamic fundamentalistic nations and Malaysian Islamic parties such as the PAS/Dar al Arquam/ABIM cannot be under estimated. Muslim nations like Egypt or Jordan which have taken a moderate or even neutral stance in the Israeli issue are the target of much hostility even from their own nationals, directed especially against their moderate regimes due to their what the fundamentalists view as pro-Israeli policies. The Malaysian regime has taken a clear anti-Israeli stand, banning entry of Israelis into Malaysia etc. and no doubt this is partly due to the pressure from the Islamic parties and the need to appease the general feeling among the Malaysian Muslims regarding the Palestinian issue

The word *dawah* though it literally means the call, signifying the call to Islam, is nevertheless not just about gaining more converts to Islam. It stands for the purifying Islam of its syncretistic elements and restoring it to the pristine purity of the Prophet's times. Traditionally Malaysian Islam has been well known for its folk nature, its integration of indigenous and pre-Islamic Hindu/Buddhist traditions with Islam. K.M. Endicott in his well known monograph *Malay Magic* [8] has made a detailed analysis of Malay folk religion, much of which is strictly speaking incompatible with Islam. Most of the Malay Ulama who had visited and perhaps studied Arabic and Islam in Saudi Arabia and other centres of

Islamic scholarship, came back fired by the zeal for purifying Malay Islam and transforming it to the Arab model which conforms more rigourously to the injunctions of the Qur'an and the Hadith and the *Shariah*. They would look at the folk practice of Islam in Malaysia as *bida* (innovation) and even as *kufr* (disbelief). The influence of these Islamic puritans was especially felt in the urban centres and among the educated youth. In the more ethnically and religiously pluralistic character of the cities the need to emphasise the distinctiveness of Malay identity is greater, which as discussed in the last chapter depends increasingly on Islam. Thus the religious aspect of this identity had to be reinforced by turning to a purer form of Islam, than in the kampongs where a more relaxed and syncretistic model of the faith would be sufficient, and have no adverse consequences. Moreover the educated youth are more conscious of the backwardness of the Malay, as well as the deficiencies of the nation such as corruption, the dependence on the West and the intrusion and rapid dissemination of Western culture, values and "moral decadence". Islam to them seems to be the panacea for the evils of Malay society and its backwardness. Hence the call for islamicisation of the state and religious revival and reform by youth movements such as the ABIM. The adoption of stricter Islamic provisions of the *Shariah* in religious practice and dress by university educated youth, especially women, and greater zeal and stricter adherence to the *Ibadah*, the rituals of Islam are symptomatic of their aspirations. This search for identity and their destiny by the urban Malay/Muslim and for a solution to the ills of Malay society led them to Islam, especially to Islam of the Wahabi fundamentalist model. The teachings of Ayatollah Khomeini, the Shiite leader and Abul Ala Mawdudi of Pakistan, Wahabi ideologue, fired them. The revolution in Iran and its anti- western polemics inspired them. This was in complete contrast to the relaxed, liberal and tolerant type of the Malay/Muslim world view of the Kampongs.

The Islamic parties would aspire to the wholesale implementation of the *Shariah* in the country. They decry the partial application of Islamic law, in which it has jurisdiction only over Muslims, which as Ustad Kipli of the Religious Affairs Department of Sarawak, and Mohammed Tawfeek of BINA told me, many consider to be unfair to Muslims. The Islamic groups criticise the piecemeal approach of the government to Islam, its separation of religion from politics, its alliance with non-Islamic political parties such as the MCA and MIC, (9) its tacit if not overt support for secularisation as opposed to the establishment of a theocratic state. The UMNO however is quite cautious in its approach to the issue of Islamicisation. It is to be remembered that while the Tunku, the Father of the Nation was a keen missionary of Islam and founder of the evangelistic organisation PERKIM, he was at the outset opposed to the establishment of even a department of Religious affairs and the *Shariah* courts. The Tunku understood that in the strongly multi-religious structure of Malaysian society, the establishment of an Islamic state would be likely to have explosive repercussions. Speaking in 1990 at the annual general meeting of Wanita Perkim he warned that religion should be a unifying force and not a tool for conflicts. (10)

The existence of the department of Religious Affairs and the Makamah *Shariah*, the Islamic Courts, is a source of apprehension to the Christians of Sarawak. From my conversations with them, It seemed to emerge that the looming threat of the Islamicisation of the state and the apprehension of the application of Islamic law to non-Muslims seem very real to them. Already many in the Islamic parties contend that when *khalwat* is alleged both partners in the offence, even if one is non- Muslim, should be prosecuted. In other words, the law regarding close proximity in the *Shariah* should be made applicable to Muslim and non- Muslim alike. There is also a proposal that the powers of the *Shariah* courts be increased. The maximum penalties have already been increased from fines of $1000 to $5000, and from six months' imprisonment to three years.(11) It is significant that some of the powers of the native courts in Sarawak which used to have jurisdiction over matters concerning Muslim Law have now been transferred to Makamah *Shariah*. (12) Jusoh Hamid, a distinguished University lecturer in Islamic law, argues that before the coming of the British the multi racial society of Malakka subsisted in perfect harmony under Islamic law. (13) As stated in the Introduction, Hajee Tawfeek of BINA also expressed similar sentiments, opining that the Islamic state would be fair to all. (14) Jusoh adds:

> People should be informed that the law of the land before the interference of British colonial rule was Islamic law. Therefore after independence, Islamic law should have been realised in the society as had been done before that (15)

The demographic peculiarities of Sarawak would most likely preclude, unlike West Malaysia, that the promulgation of an Islamic state in Malaysia would find much support among the indigenous inhabitants. It is to be remembered that Sarawak is the only state in Malaysia where Islam is still not accepted as the official religion. However in 1991 the then Minister for Industrial Development, Haji Openg, did predict that Sarawak would be the first state in Malaysia to implement the *Shariah* for Muslims. [16] In spite of its minority character, the Muslims of Sarawak seem to still aspire for the supremacy of Islam in the state. However as with the UMNO in the peninsula, the leadership in Sarawak seem to be quite moderate and tactful in its support for Islamicisation. Speaking in 1991, Chief Minister Taib Mohammed stated that the State government will assist the Federal Administration in all efforts to promote unity and harmony among Malaysians. [17] Speaking at the Chinese New Year function in Sibu he stressed the multi- racial character of the Barisan National Government which would be the most beneficial for the country. [18] He warned that the country will be thrown into chaos if the government yielded to pressure from one race.[19] Tun Abang Openg, the Minister for Industrial Development speaking at Kampung Tebun stressed that the government would strive for the progress and development of the rakyat (proletariat) irrespective of their racial origins and religious beliefs. [20] At the Annual Delegations Meeting of the BINA, in September 1993 the Chief Minister advised the organisation to be discreet in their *dawah* activities pointing out that "there is no force in Islam". [21] However, the splendour of the Department of Religious Affairs, the Makamah *Shariah* with an Islamic library attached to the Department, the state Mosques etc. testify to the high financial support that the state government accords, and the great importance attached by the state administration to these Islamic institutions, which seem quite disproportionate in view of the demographic patterns of Sarawak.

On the other hand Reverend Aries spoke of hurdles placed by the bureaucracy on the construction of churches, acquisition of land for the purpose and such strategies for hindering the work of the Church.

As with the Education Department, I experienced some difficulty in getting to meet officials of the Department of Religious Affairs. The chief officers seemed quite evasive and though appointments were made to see me they were not kept. Finally, I managed to meet Ustad Kipli, a rather Junior Official, I suspect. A graduate of the University Kebangsan in Islamic studies, Ustad Kipli is a young, intelligent and friendly individual. However his statement that the Government encouraged the revival of all religions, seemed to be more the language of diplomacy and tact than the truth. The fact is that the government's support of Islam and Islamic institutions and its encouragement to revivalist and proselytising Islamic agencies have created a reaction among the Hindu, Buddhist and other religious communities, stimulating a revivalist response in them. Mr. Kipli was of the view that the status of Islam as a state religion (yet to come about in Sarawak) does not confer any special rights on Muslims, but on the other hand is in some respects disadvantageous to them as only they are subject to the rather rigourous stipulations of the *Shariah*. However, his attestation of government neutrality in religious matters seemed to me to be expression of a democratic ideal rather than a fact.

The more aggressive of the Islamic parties such as PAS, and Dar al Arquam are not very active in Sarawak -- I have given a resume of the various political parties of Sarawak in appendix 1. Dr. Tan Chee Beng opines that the UMNO is the Islamic party in the BN federal government.[22] If so the Parti Bhumiputera consisting mainly of the Malay/Melanau political faction led by Taib Muhammed is its counterpart in Sarawak and thus the Islamic party of the state administration. The Chief Minister is a Melanau/Muslim and does encourage the propagation and revival of Islam in the country and Sarawak, though he clearly advocates discreet and gentler methods of revival and proselytisation. As Col. Dunstan Nynaring, a political secretary to the Chief Minister, told me, the government is moderate and extremism is not encouraged. Speaking at the inaugural ceremony of the 11th Annual Delegations Meet of BINA in September. 1991 Chief Minister Taib stated:

> Members of the Islamic *dawah* should not aim to convert as many people as possible to be Muslims without taking into consideration the consequences which would surface later on [23]

He also pointed out that there is no force in Islam and the *dawah* movement must be carried out in discreet (sic) and with tact so that the religion is better understood by people of other races. [24] Evidently he sees eye to eye with Dr. Mahathir in this issue who has warned extremists that they give Islam a bad name, a sentiment echoed by Ustad Muhammad Mortadza Haji Dawd, President of BINA who stated at the same function that: "Islam has recently been branded as a religion belonging to fundamentalists, extremists and the anti-social".[25]

However Taib Muhammed is one of the founding members of BINA which is essentially an Islamic revivalist and proselytising institution. The state government had given 600,000 to PERKIM, the national Islamic organisation,[26] (BINA is the offshoot of the PERKIM in Sarawak). The grandeur and magnificence of the new BINA headquarters in Kuching could certainly not have been achieved by a charitable organisation without state support. The BINA brochure does say that building materials for over 20 mosques were donated by the state government. It is clear that in line with the policy of the UMNO in peninsular Malaysia and the Malay/Melanau Muslim group and also in conformity with the general aspirations of the Malay/Muslims of the nation, the PBB led by Taib Muhammed has been favouring the Muslims of Sarawak and their institutions, in spite of the minority character of the Islamic community in the state. This is reflected also in the gradually increasing dominant position of Muslims in the bureaucracy and other positions of responsibility and power. Though Colonel Dunstan tends to portray it as a natural consequence of the Muslim leadership of the government stating that they would like to " have people from their own community around them" and condones this favouritism to some extent, non- Muslims would view such actions as discrimination, pure and simple. The Christians seem to be especially incensed since other than the tribal religions, their faith is the numerically preponderant in Sarawak.

BINA is an offshoot of PERKIM,[27] the missionary organisation founded in 1960 by Tunku as a national level religious organisation unaffiliated to any State Religious Council, but directly under the Prime Minister's control. Its links with the government means that it generally follows the UMNO/PBB policies on Islam, avoiding extremism, adopting a soft touch in its conversion and Islamicising programmes, and being much more liberal in its application of Islamic law in comparison to the rigorous approach of the other *dawah* organisations such as ABIM and Dar al Arquam. The latter have not been able to get much of a foothold in Sarawak, a fact which has had a salutary effect on Christian-Muslim relations. I met Haji Mohammed Tawfeek Sahran, the Chief Executive Secretary of BINA in his spacious and comfortable office in the splendorous new headquarters of BINA at Petra Jaya which reputedly cost $5 million to build. The complex includes a library, a school for new converts for instruction in Islam and a hall which can accommodate an audience of 2000 etc. However the complex is still considered incomplete as it needs a hostel for new converts to comprehensively meet the needs of BINA's activities.

Haji Tawfeek, as he is popularly known, is an extremely pleasant and friendly individual, easily accessible and patient, informative and unevasive in his answers to my questions. He is no doubt an extremely competent and effective ambassador for BINA. His answers generally reflected not only PERKIM's commitment to Islam but its tolerance of other faiths and its non- dogmatic approach to Islamic rules and regulations, especially to those of a symbolic nature such as adoption of Arab dress and customs, and the use of Jawi script (the script originating in Java, i.e. Arabic script). According to Tawfeek the question of dress etc. in Islam is rather superficial and the real revival is in the heart. It is to be noted that PERKIM does not insist on circumcision of converts and even does not compel forest-dwelling Orang Asli to abandon consumption of wild pig/boar, as this is perhaps the only food available for them in their nowadays reduced habitat .[28] It is to be remembered that to the ABIM, Dar al Arquam etc. these outward manifestations of adherence to the

Shariah is quite important. The reversion to Islamic dress, which exposes only the face and hands in the case of women, and stipulates green/white turban and robes for men (Dar al Arquam) according to Tawfeek are not the essential element of revival. *Dawah* should counter the increasing secularisation and materialism of the nation.

However the Islamicisation of the state seems to be the ultimate goal of BINA as with the more fundamentalist organisations. Haji Tawfeek admitted to this aspiration, but conceded that such Islamicisation will be a long process. He admitted that matters like banking etc. have to be worked out. He opined that promulgation of the *Shariah* will be beneficial to non-Muslims. The Islamic state would be quite fair to them. He pointed to the experience of Islamic states in medieval times. But even the first Islamic state Yathrib (Madina) had its problems. In spite of the fairness and egalitarianism of the Prophet's constitution for the first ever Islamic state the Jews did not accept the supremacy of Islam and had to be driven out. Even some of the *Ansar* (helpers, original inhabitants of Madina) were not happy.

Evidently BINA works towards the goal of the Islamic state, probably cherished by all Malay/Muslims since it will be the inevitable conclusion of their aspiration for ascendancy, the religious factor gradually overtaking the ethnic dimension. However its *modus operandi* is quite different from that of ABIM, Dar al Arquam etc. Negata opines that PERKIM is slowly working for the clear numerical superiority of Islam in the nation which at present is marginal and certainly does not confer on Islam an absolute demographic majority.[29] Unlike the fundamentalist parties it acknowledges the extremely ethnically and religiously pluralistic nature of Malaysia and the present inadvisability of Islamicising the State. The opportune moment for declaring the Islamic state would be when Islam is incontrovertibly superior numerically. Their advocacy of considering non-Malay converts to Islam as Malay/Bhumiputra and their efforts to obtain allowances, concessions and privileges for them become clear in the light of this long term objective. Evidently for the Tunku, as I have stated earlier, Islam has supplanted ethnicity as the criterion for Malayness. The adoption of PERKIM ideology in their proselytising activities and attitudes to the *Saudara Baru* (new brothers i.e. new converts to

Islam) seems to be in conformity with this fact. The pronouncements of some of the Sarawak ministers reflect the same views on *dawah*. Speaking in March 1990, Deputy Chief Minister Sim Cheng Hong advised that the promotion of religion should be based on the concept of multi-racialism [30] Speaking at the opening of the new state Mosque at Kuching in December 1990, Chief Minister Taib Mohammed called for Muslims to practice equality as required by Islam so that there will be no barriers based on colour, status and wealth. [31]

Negata is quite correct in pointing out that Perkim is not hostile to modernisation nor even to Western culture. [32] This is in conformity with the attitudes of the UMNO and especially Prime Minister Dr. Mahathir. In his book *The Challenge* Dr. Mahathir seeks to impress upon Malaysians the need for Western scientific and technological education. He points to instances such as Islamic Spain which became weak, and where Islam was supplanted by Christianity as a consequence of not acquiring such knowledge. [33] Though he decries Western trends in dress, morality etc, he states that knowledge in science and technology and dynamic progress in these areas of learning are necessary for the survival of Islam. He points out that what is called Western knowledge had its origins in Islam, citing the names of Ibn Sina (Medicine), al Kwarizini (Mathematics), Ibn al Haythan (Physics) etc.[34] Thus he seeks to underplay the contrasts between Islamic and European knowledge. The Islamic parties have always sought to foster hostility against modern scientific and technical knowledge and Western education which they depict as against Islamic beliefs (e.g. the Theory of Evolution). BINA however seems to toe the line set by Dr. Mahathir. Chief Minister Taib Muhammad, one of the founders of BINA, in his inaugural speech at the 11th Annual Delegations Meeting of the BINA exhorted Muslims to be dynamic and progressive and to acquire modern knowledge and skills. He stated:

> Islam is a religion which prompts a better living and way
> of life for humans on earth and in the afterworld. One
> way of achieving a better living standard and status is for
> the Muslims to equip themselves with knowledge and

skills which would make them a progressive and dynamic community in a modern setting. (35)

Such an attitude to Western education would also promote better relations with Christians, since as in India and other former European colonies there has been a tendency to associate the Christian citizens with the colonial masters on the basis of their common religion, and also since in those times the Christians seemed to be more Westernised than their compatriots belonging to other faiths. The Christian Churches and their style of worship project a mainly western image. This perspective of non-Christians of associating the Christians with the West has tended to linger on in post-Independence times. It is to be remembered that not very long ago, Devi Lal, the then Deputy Prime Minister of India stated publicly that the Indian Christians are aliens and should migrate to Europe or America.

This association of Christians with the West is particularly strong in the minds of Muslims and other non-Christian faiths in connection with the field of education, since the Christian schools were the pioneers of the Western education system in Malaysia and other former European colonial territories. However unlike other Islamic organisations PERKIM/BINA does not decry Western education and knowledge in toto.

Most of the proselytising activities of BINA seem to be targetted at the tribal indigenous groups, Iban, Melanau, Bidayuh etc. Rev. Aries Sumping, Principal of the Kuching Anglican Theological College, remarked that there was not much missionary activity by Muslims among the Christians, probably in deference to the prohibition against Christians trying to convert Muslims. However the BINA brochure does mention Christian converts to Islam e.g. two BINA health workers, Abdul Khalid Nicholas and Ayub Abdul Rahman, the latter none other than a former Roman Catholic priest! (36) Some Christians told me that BINA has converted Christians to Islam offering financial inducements, but I cannot say how true this allegation is. BINA also works among the Chinese and presumably among Chinese Christians. The BINA brochure mentions the encroaching influences of Christian Missionary activities as one of the problems that new converts, presumably tribals, face (37) Thus though there may be not overt confrontation between Christian evangelists and the BINA it seems that they might be in keen competition with each other among the indigenous Sarawak tribes. BINA states that Islam is easily acceptable to them, because of the simplicity of its teachings, a statement that seems to subtly imply that those of the Christian faith are not. (38)

In spite of the contrasts in their ideologies, BINA states that it works closely with ABIM. (39) Of course the former prominent ABIM leader Anwar Ibrahim is part of the UMNO administration. Many members of the ABIM feel that Anwar's joining the UMNO was not a defection but rather an infiltration of the UMNO for transforming its ideology and policy from within (40) ABIM is of course one of the more moderate *dawah* organisations and has recently been less critical of the Government than PAS, Dar al Arquam etc.(41) Among the objectives of BINA listed in their brochure is the rather enigmatic statement that it will establish "close rapport, mediations and cooperation with Islamic organisations and bodies in Malaysia in respect to matters relating to Islamic advancement". (43) The word "mediations" seems to indicate that BINA would seek no confrontation with the fundamentalist and extremist organisations. It is significant that of late the UMNO administration has also toned down its recrimination of the Islamic parties, probably as I have stated elsewhere in recognition of the strong appeal that Islam and *dawah* have for the Malay/Muslim population especially the educated youth. BINA is a useful tool in the hands of the UMNO in its new policy of strengthening the Malay/Muslim equation and countering the allegation of the more extremist Islamic organisations that it is unIslamic and supportive of ethnic separatism (*asabiyya*).

It would seem that the Sarawak State Government as the Federal Government, is not keen on Islamicising the state immediately, but as Haji Tawfeek opined would like it to be a long term process and entered into gradually after ensuring the right circumstances viz. the ensuring of a substantial Muslim majority in the state by conversions to Islam, the establishment of strong Islamic institutions, the gradual extension and intensification of *Shariah* through the Department of Religious Affairs and the *Shariah* courts, the strengthening of an Islamic ethos in schools, and the dominance of Islam in public life through Islamic symbols in public functions and celebration of national days, as also the closer integration of Sarawak into the Federation and such moves designed to counter the present numerically inferior status of the Malay/Muslims in the state.

It is apparent that in spite of its different demographic structure the experience of the non Malay/non-Muslim in Sarawak is not very much different from that of Peninsular Malaysia. It is true that the more fundamentalist and rigourous Muslim parties such as the PAS and Dar al Arquam are not very popular in the state. However the *dawah* movement in the state seems to be on the whole successful and gaining momentum both by way of a revival among Muslims and in gaining new converts. The support of the state government leadership, the use of state funds and the unity of the Malay/Muslim population are essential for the promotion and assertion of Islam in Sarawak, where demographically Islam and the Malays have only a lower status, lower than the Christians and the animists in the religious, and lower than the Ibans and the Chinese in the ethnic configurations. The inevitable infiltration of the policies and attitudes of the peninsula due to Sarawak's membership of the Federation also aids the ascendency of the Muslims. The Federal Government supports *dawah* and the strengthening of Islamic institutions through financial support, and visits and encouragement by Federal leaders. It is significant that the state administration is a Muslim-led coalition and that Taib Muhammad is very much in sympathy with the policies of UMNO and Dr. Mahathir, having been a Cabinet Minister and long-time associate of the federal leaders. The fact that he walked out of a meeting (at Bintulu during the 20th Anniversary of Malaysian independance) in protest against his own uncle the former Chief Minister, Abdul Rahman Yakub's criticism of the Federal administration reveals his loyalty to and support for Dr. Mahathir's policies. (44) Thus in spite of the demographic contrasts, the policies of the state leadership ensures the hegemony of Islam in Christian majority Sarawak.

As the government's agency for *dawah* and for its policy of strengthening Islam, BINA has a gentle non-aggressive touch as contrasted with other agencies for Islamic revival in Malaysia, though its long term ambition would be the same as theirs, namely *Dar - al- Islam*. However muted and tactful it might be, the promotion of Islam makes the Muslim population aware of their religious identity, and both its potentiality for dominance in the state owing to the support of the Federal and State administration and its vulnerability due to its inferior numerical status. This provokes a greater impetus for revival and resurgence and for Islamic proselytisation. The Malay/Muslims of Sarawak are conscious of these factors, and would seek to assert their strength in all ways possible, whether in the educational field by insisting on the teaching of Islam as opposed to other faiths, or the strengthening of Islamic institutions, the building of new mosques, *sauras* (prayer houses) and madrasas (religious schools), the enhancement of the Makamah *Shariah* and the Department of Religious Affairs, and the projection of Islamic symbols in national days, national celebrations, state functions and other aspects of civil life. In addition as Col. Dunstan mentions there might be an informal networking of Malay/Muslims in the state bureaucracy, and consequent favouritism shown to the Malay/Muslims in official appointments, postings, promotion etc. The minority status of the Malay/Muslim seems to promote greater solidarity in Sarawak than would have been the case, and might stimulate a more assertive stance. I have observed this phenomenon, for instance, in the Lakshadweep Islands, where the native population is almost one hundred percent Muslim, but the Hindus, who are a vast majority on mainland India and who in earlier days used to be in charge of key areas of the administration, were more aggressively assertive of their authority here than anywhere on the mainland and an informal networking to this end was operative. This is both a defensive reaction to their vulnerable position as numerically inferior and a quest to impose their numerically dominant position on the mainland in this region as well, where in reality they are demographically not in that status. I have no direct experience or facts but have a feeling that this complex psychology operates also among the Hindu employees/Federal police/armed forces in other Indian States where they are a minority, for instance in Kashmir and the Punjab. The situation of the Malay/Muslim in Sarawak is perhaps analogous to the situation and attitudes of the Hindu in Lakshadweep. But the Malay/Muslim in coalition with the Melanau is a substantial segment of the Sarawak population, and unlike the Hindus in the afore-mentioned Indian states, a force to be reckoned with. Therefore the *dawah* process and the Islamic assertion is quite a significant factor in Sarawak for inter-religious relations and especially Christian-Muslim relations, since Christianity is demographically the biggest religious sector of the population in this state.

Notes

9.   M.C.A.= Malaysian Chinese Association.
     M.I.C.= Malaysian Indian Congress.
26. PERKIM= Pertubuhan Kebaajikan Islam Malaysia (Islamic Welfare and Missionary Association of Malaysia).

References

1. Khomeini, Ayatullah (1979), "An Islamic State - Point of View" in Islamic Council of Europe, *Concept of Islamic State*, I.C.E.: London, pp. 5-7, p. 7.
2. Mohammed, Mahathir (1986), *The Challenge*, Petaling Jeya, Pelanduk Publications: Petaling Jeya, p. 55.
3. Merad, Ali (1981), "The ideologisation of Islam in the Contemporary World', in Cudsi, A.S., and Dessouki, A.E.H., *Islam and Power*, Croom Helm: London, pp. 37-48, p. 44.
4. Chapter Two, p. 17.
5. Sundaram, J.K., and Cheek, A.S. (April, 1988), "The Politics of Malaysia's Islamic Resurgence", *Third World Quarterly* 10, No. 2, pp. 843-868, p. 856.
6. Ibid., p. 867.
7. Shacht, Joseph (1964), *An Introduction to Islamic Law*, Clarendon Press: Oxford, p. 79.
8. Endicott, K.M. (1970), *An Analysis of Malay Magic*, Oxford University Press: Singapore.
10. *Sarawak Gazette*, September 1990, p. 43.

11. Jusoh, Hamid (1991), *The Position of Islamic Law in the Malaysian Constitution*, Dewan Bahasa dan Pustaka Kementerian Pendidikan Malaysia: Kuala Lumpur, p. 48.

12. Ibid., p. 103.

13. Ibid., pp. 96 and 102.

14. Ibid., p. 102.

15. *Sarawak Gazette*, July 1991, p. 44.

16. *Sarawak Gazette*, April 1991, p. 60.

17. Ibid., p. 62.

18. *Sarawak Gazette*, December 1989, p. 52.

19. *Sarawak Gazette*, September 1990, p. 47.

20. *Sunday Tribune*, Kuching, 19th September 1993.

21. Khoon Tan Chee, *Malaysia Today*, Petaling Jeya, Pelanduk Publications, 1985, p.14.

22. *Sunday Tribune*, 18th September 1993.

23. Ibid.

24. Ibid.

25. *Sarawak Gazette*, June 1982, p.59.

27. Negata, Judith (1984), *The Reflowering of Malaysian Islam*, University of British Columbia Press: Vancouver

28. Ibid., p. 173.

29. *Sarawak Gazette*, April 1990, p.43.

30. *Sarawak Gazette*, December 1990, p. 65.

31. Negata op.cit., p. 171.

32. Mohammed, Mahathir, op. cit., p. 36.

33. Ibid., p. 32.

34. *Sunday Tribune*, Kuching, 19th September, 1993.

35. Angkatan Nahadathul Islam Bersatu (1993), *BINA, A Brief Introduction*, BINA: Kuching, p.6.

36. Ibid., p. 7.

37. Ibid.

38. Ibid.

39. Ibid.

40. Sundaram and Cheek, Op. cit., p. 856.

41. Ibid., p. 560.

42. *BINA, A Brief Introduction*, p. 4.

43. See Ching, Yu Loon (1987) *Sarawak, The Plot that Failed*, Summer Times Publishing: Singapore, p. 3.

5 Spreading the truth: The Christian experience

The Christian Church in Malaysia has a long history going back right up to the 16th century when the Portuguese established the Roman Catholic church in Melakka. The first church was built on St. Paul's hill by Albuquerque the redoubtable Portuguese admiral in 1521.[1]

The history of the church in Sarawak is more recent, dating back to 1841 when the state was founded by James Brooke, the English sailor who became the Rajah of Sarawak on 24th September 1841. Earlier contacts with Christianity were sporadic, and did not last long. It is said that one Father Pereira had visited Borneo in 1608 and had suggested to his superiors that Borneo was a fertile field for Christian mission. However there was no response from Portugal and eventually the Sultan of Brunei, apprehensive of this intrusion of Christianity in his domain, sent Father Pereira away. The worthy Father is believed to have drowned in this voyage. In 1688 another Catholic visitor, this time from Sicily, visited Borneo and converted some natives, but as in the case of Father Pereira the Sultan of Brunei is said to have put an end to his proselytising activities. [2] The more sustained and substantial efforts at evangelisation thus commenced during the Brooke regime, and was mainly due to the efforts of

James Brooke, the first Rajah, himself. The Brookes encouraged the establishment of Churches and missionary work, but their attitude to the church was rather pragmatic. They viewed the work of the church as a civilising and "pacifying" influence on the indigenous population rather than as benefiting them spiritually. Christianity was however to become an important religion in Sarawak.

The established missionary organisations were in the beginning reluctant to take on the evangelisation of as remote and difficult a region as Borneo, so a new missionary organisation, the Borneo Church Mission Institution was founded to undertake the task. (3) Rev F. T. McDougall, physician and minister became the first Anglican missionary to Sarawak. He was later to become the first Bishop of Labuan. Due to paucity of funds the Borneo Mission was later on taken over by the S.P.G. (Society for the Propagation of the Gospel) The S.P.G. was thus one of the first international missions to work in Sarawak, beginning its activities in 1854. (4)

The establishment of schools by the church was especially important to the Brookes as the means by which Western scientific and technological knowledge became accessible to the natives. The St. Thomas and St. Mary schools of Kuching established in 1867 were the first Mission schools to function in Sarawak. The churches in Peninsular Malaysia were under the jurisdiction of Bishops in India, but Sarawak had its own Anglican Bishop, stationed at the island of Labuan, whose leadership was later extended to the Peninsula and Singapore. The Roman Catholic church and the Methodists followed the Anglicans in 1855 and 1901 respectively. The now defunct Borneo Evangelical mission (B.E.M.) founded in 1928 by three young Australians was another of the pioneering missions who evangelised among the forest dwelling tribes of Sarawak, centring their activities near the Limbang river area. (5)

In spite of the lack of commitment on the part of the Brooke administration, their utilitarian view of the Church's mission, and their reluctance to upset the traditions and social order of the indigenous tribes, the Church in Sarawak has prospered. The strong and flourishing churches in Kuching and other cities and the fact that the Christians are the biggest religious group in the state testifies to its growth. Roy Bruton states that Christian advance in Sarawak has been much more significant than the Muslim. (6) This is probably due to the fact that the consciousness of the Malay/Muslim identity has emerged and strengthened mainly after independence from colonial rule. The *dawah* movement in Islam is of fairly recent origin, or at least it has intensified only in recent years, whereas Christian commitment to evangelisation was at a peak in earlier years and remains unabated though the lack of governmental approval and even discouragement, and restrictive measures instituted by them might be stifling the proselytisation activities nowadays. The momentum generated during the British days, when the Brooke administration and later the colonial regime, though their support was not unequivocal, was at least not obstructive of Christian evangelisation, has been sustained in Sarawak by committed European and native Christian workers. Rev. Aries Sumping, Principal of the Kuching Anglican Theological College told me that while there is very little evangelisation by Christians in West Malaysia, the Church in Sarawak is still active in mission and converting. As a matter of fact in view of the prohibition on proselytising among Muslims, extant from colonial times, the Christian missionary field in peninsular Malaysia is restricted to the Hindus, Buddhists and other non- Muslim communities among the immigrant population, and to the Orang Asli and other tribal groups. Evangelisation among the aborigines of the peninsula was viewed with alarm by the rulers and the Malay religious leaders who considered the tribals as potential Muslims. As a result the Christian Church refrained from proselytising and confined their work to medical, agriculture and educational assistance to the non-Muslims. Thus in reality there is very little missionary work in the Peninsula among even these groups. Sarawak and Sabah where the non-Malay/Muslim groups are substantial remain the main missionary field of the Christian Church in Malaysia. In peninsular Malaysia 'alien' Christian missionaries, including those who are natives of East Malaysia are banned from visiting the aboriginal territories. Gordon P. Means states that the government officials working in the Tribal Affairs Department (Jabatan Orang Asli) induce the aborigines by subtle means to become Muslim, promising them the special privileges and concessions given to Malays. Aboriginal Christians are also said to be intimidated by Departmental officials when they try to conduct Christian worship in the aboriginal areas. [7] The government has powers to exclude any kind of written material from the tribal regions. In Sarawak however, a large number of indigenous groups such as the Iban and the Bidayuh are no longer forest dwellers, and are in fact part of a highly developed society. Many of them have converted to Christianity.

The Malay/Muslim population and the UMNO who represent them in the Federal administration seem to be quite concerned about the demographic structure of the country and keen to maintain the numerical superiority of the Malay/Muslims. They are particularly concerned about Christian evangelisation as the other non-Muslim faiths of Malaysia such as the Hindus are not so committed to proselytisation as the Christians. There was a furore when a Christian book store imported some copies of Bibles from Indonesia which were translations of the Bible into the Malay language. The customs officials impounded copies of *Al Kitab* which was later on banned by the government on the grounds that it used words like "Allah" and " Nabi" which the administration felt were properly to be used only by Muslims. This also meant that hymnals and liturgical books and other Christian literature which made use of similar terms could not be imported from Indonesia. Gordon P. Means opines that this regulation amounted to a retroactive ban on all existing Christian literature which made use of the 25 words and 9 expressions referred to by the Government. (8) It is significant that Dr. Tan Chee Khoon considers Indonesia, though it is now an Islamic state, properly and officially declared, to be much more tolerant to the Christian faith. (9) Among the reasons given by Dr. Khoon for this opinion is the fact that Indonesia does not prohibit the publication and sale of Christian literature making use of "Islamic" terms. Christian protestations against these, to them totally unwarranted and unjustifiable restrictions, resulted in the partial lifting of the ban, approved translations of the Bible and other literature being permitted to be used by them. (10) The *al Kitab* was allowed to be imported to East Malaysia, probably in view of the fact that the region is a Christian majority area.

The ban on the *al Kitab* and use of Islamic words is a significant and controversial issue in Christian-Muslim relations in Malaysia. The use of the Bible, liturgy, hymnal etc. in the Bahasa is quite crucial to the Christians, since the promotion of Bahasa Malaysia as the national language and its use as the sole medium of instruction in most schools mean that many Christians and potential converts can read the Bible only in the Bahasa medium. It is strange that on the one hand the government is keen to promote the Bahasa as the national language, ostensibly to forge national unity, but probably also to underwrite the prominence of the Malay ethnic group (since the Malay language is the major component of Bahasa Malaysia), but then prevented the Christians from using that language for their religious activities. It should not be overlooked that the sharing of religious terms by Christians and Muslims also emphasise their common scriptural and doctrinal roots and would be helpful in promoting Christian -Muslim dialogue and good relations.

The word *Allah* in Arabic is a compound word which can be separated into the components *al Ilah* which simply means "The God". It affirms the intensely monotheistic nature of Islamic belief that rejects the concept of other Gods. The use of the definite article precludes the very existence of any other divine beings. However Muslims accept that the God they worship is none other than the God of Abraham, Isaac and Jacob, namely the God of the Jewish and Christian faiths. There may be differences in nomenclature and the understanding of the nature and qualities of God between the three religions e. g. the Christian concept of the Trinity, but there is no doubt that it is the same Being that the three religions worship. The word *Allah* is related to the Hebrew term *Elohim* for God. The fact that both Christians and Muslims worship the same God, and that unlike the words *Jehovah* or *Siva* the term *Allah* is not a specific name for the Deity but only the Arabic for God makes the Christian use of the word quite innocuous and legitimate. The Sikhs in Malaysia also use the same term when they refer to God, though there is some doubt that the Sikhs consider *Akal* their deity as the same as Jehovah and Allah.

The Muslim apprehension seems to rest only on the probability that some Muslims may be attracted to the Christian faith when they see familiar words to which they have a sentimental attachment used by the Christians for God, prophet etc. The UMNO administration and the Malay/Muslim would see use of what they consider to be essentially Islamic terminology as an attempt to mislead and confuse Muslims and divert them away from commitment to their own faith.

They probably see such actions as an attempt to circumvent the prohibition on proselytising Muslims. The Christians could very well be totally innocent of any such intentions, but for the UMNO and the Malay/Muslim the chances of a Muslim coming into contact with the teaching of the Bible would be greater if the book was available in their own language. There is a prohibition in law against selling or gifting non-Muslim religious tracts or other literature to a Muslim unless he specifically requests for the same. Similarly Christian/non-Muslim preaching in public is prohibited (however in Sarawak recently this was permitted on Christmas day). A Muslim who voluntarily attends a regularly conducted Christian service in a church or other institution is liable to punishment under *Shariah* law, though the Christians in charge of the service are not deemed culpable because a Muslim attended them. There are also restrictions on films which convey a Christian message or even extol a non-Muslim religious figure, or one which decries Muslim beliefs or offends Muslim religious sensibilities. In British times religious services of all the major faiths were broadcast over Radio Malaya. However nowadays only Muslim worship is broadcast over the radio and Television (In Sarawak a short Christian service is allowed to be broadcast on Sundays). Non-Muslim religions are allowed one or two broadcasts on their important religious days, but the script of the broadcast has to be approved by the government prior to transmission. However Qur'an reading, lectures on Islamic law and doctrines etc. are regularly broadcast. The whole field of literature and the media seem to be heavily biassed on the side of Islam.

The above facts are suggestive of two important aspects of the politicisation of religion which is increasingly coming to be a prominent feature of Malaysian public life in recent times. One, the paranoia which surrounds the Malay/Muslim consciousness regarding their numerical superiority which they wish to safeguard at all costs. This is reminiscent of the feelings expressed by some Hindus in India that they are declining in numbers as a result of Christian proselytisation, and indeed that they are a dying race. Secondly, it is indicative of the increasing supplanting of the ethnic by the religious element in the Malay/Muslim identity which I referred to in Chapter 3. [11] In Malaysia as well as in India, during the undemocratic and autocratic period of the colonial regime the question of demographic superiority of one race/religion against the others was not very significant or relevant. But after independence the majority principle on which the democratic form of government rested implied that the question of numbers became very important. The Muslims of British India, were quick to see this consequence of the institution of democratic government and clamoured for and obtained separation from what they perceived as Hindu majority India. Malaysia witnessed on the eve of independence and in Post-Merdeka times a stimulation and crystallization of Malay consciousness, which under the increased Islamic resurgence of recent times is fast being supplanted by the idea of the Malay/Muslim equation and the prominence of the religious over the ethnic dimension of the equation.

Educational institutions are one of the most important avenues for the Christian church in their evangelisation endeavours. They also established hospitals and other social care establishments and even small scale industries where they could contact non- Christians and communicate the Gospel to them. But the best forum they had for spreading knowledge of the Christian faith was through their religious instruction classes. School assemblies where prayers would be said and a passage from the scriptures read and even a short homily delivered also afforded opportunities for exposing the children to Christian teaching. In colonial times all students irrespective of their religious background attended these assemblies and religious instruction/Bible knowledge classes. Of course non-Christian parents were free to take their children out of these classes, but in India as a matter of fact they rarely did. Roy Bruton states that in Sarawak, there was no significant Malay enrolment in Mission schools owing to the objection of Muslim parents to the above-mentioned activities. (12) Rev. Aries however informed me that many of the Muslim leaders of Sarawak were products of Mission schools. The mission school administration was very liberal, and kept their doors open to people from all faiths not only to be students, but also to be members of staff. But the majority of teachers belonged to the Christian faith and the head was invariably a member of the particular denomination which established and managed the school.

After independence there have been tremendous changes as far as mission schools are concerned. The salaries of staff and most of the day to day expenses of the schools are met by the government, so the state administration has much more control and say in the running of these schools. According to the Education Act of 1961, the Education Minister could form a committee or board to supervise the affairs of an aided school [Sec. 26 A (4))] The Minister has powers to wind up the Management Board of such schools. The committee set up by the Minister can even review and appeal to the Education Minister against the appointment of the head of an aided school, and the Minister's decision on the appeal is final (Sec. 32 A). Teachers could be dismissed from service of aided schools only on approval of the Minister of Education (Sec. 32). 75% of the staff of Christian schools are now appointed by the government. The prominence of the Malay/Muslim in the national consciousness and in policies have not left these schools alone. Mission schools taught mainly through English in former days and were indeed the pioneers of the Western mode of education in Malaysia as in most British colonies. The conversion of the medium of instruction to Malay and the institution of a national curriculum in post-Merdeka Malaysia has had a serious impact on the nature of the teaching and on the Christian ethos of these schools. Gordon P. Means points out how through direct regulations, supervision of the examination system, and the strings attached grants-in-aid system, government policies were forced on the mission and other private schools (such as Chinese schools). (13) One area to suffer the impact of the new policies is religious instruction. In 1961, the teaching of non- Muslim faiths was prohibited in all aided schools as part of the syllabus or during regular school hours. As I have mentioned in the introduction teachers being paid in full or in part from government funds cannot teach Non-Muslim faiths even on a voluntary basis. (14) On the other hand Islamic instruction became compulsory if there were more than 15 Muslim students in the schools, such instruction being given during normal school hours and usually by teachers provided by the state government--from state schools according to Ustad Kipli of the Sarawak Religious Affairs Department.

The Education Act of 1961 states that the duration of Islamic instruction should be at least two hours a week [Sec. 36(2)]. The managers or governors of the school have to see to the proper arrangements for this. Half the expenses for running these courses would be met by the Federal Government from the federal budget [Sec 37(4)] and the rest by the State Government. The Act specifically stipulates that no government funds can be spent on the religious instruction of students of non-Muslim faiths (Sec 38 a). Pupils are allowed to attend only instruction in the religion they profess (Sec 38 b). This particular stipulation effectively puts an end to all Christian proselytisation in mission schools. They are no longer the powerful tool of evangelisation that they were prior to 1961.

Dr. Tan Chee Khoon commends Christian seminaries for teaching Islam so that Christian priests have a correct understanding of what Islam is and an accurate grasp of its tenets. [15] However he alleges that the Government is reluctant to allow experts in Christian-Muslim relations from outside, who are not easily available locally, to come to Malaysia and teach in the Seminaries. He refers to the instance of the expulsion of one such expert. [16] On the other hand Islamic Civilisation is a compulsory subject in the teachers' training curriculum. Paul Ing and Teresa Ee point out that since 80% of entrants to such training are Malay/Muslims owing to privileges in selection to teachers' training and higher education for the Malays, it would stand to reason that they will predominate the school staff in the near future, and that while they would have a good grasp of Islam and its historical denouement, they will have very little knowledge or understanding of other faiths or even the inclination to acquire such knowledge. [17]

Apparently the Government has initiated in the national curricula at all levels Moral Education as an alternative to Islamic education for non- Muslim students. [18] Since Moral Education would be mostly taught by teachers who are either Muslim or who has learnt about Islamic history in the Teachers' training schools, it is inevitable that they would be teaching Moral Education from a Muslim perspective and with little authentic understanding of other faiths, preventing a balanced ideological development of the younger generation. Such a situation would not be conducive to good inter-religious relations.

Rev. Hwa Yung is of the opinion that Moral Education divorced from a religious basis would be of little value, as only religion could provide moral education with an adequate rationale. He asks why the Government could not make provision for religious education for all students in their respective faiths. (19) Evidently this would give rise to some logistical problems because of the pluralistic nature of Malaysian Society. The ideal step would be the teaching of all the major religions of Malaysia to all the students, Muslim and non-Muslim. This will go a long way towards fostering tolerance and good inter-religious relations. Part of the problem is the lack of an authentic understanding of other religions and the misconceptions and distortions which many hold of religions other than their own. Britain has initiated such an approach in their compulsory religious education lessons in British schools, though the present Conservative administration has stipulated an emphasis on the Christian faith in the syllabi for R.E and also in the collective worship activities of the school general assembly. Ing and Ee asks why the civilisation of other faiths could not be taught to Muslim teacher trainees so as to foster in them a proper understanding of their non-Muslim pupils, a pertinent and legitimate question. (20)

The Malay/Muslim population seem also to be against the more symbolic though visible expressions of other faiths. I have already mentioned the issue of bureaucrats blocking the construction of churches. Rev. Paul Chee Ing, Secretary of the MCCBHS criticises the regulation that while a population of 4000 Christians are necessary for construction of a church in a locality only 800 Muslims are needed for construction of a mosque. He calls these criteria as "unbalanced" probably implying "discriminatory". He further points out that in the structural plan for Kuala Lumpur in the year 2000 A.D., only 30% of sites of worship are for non-Muslim faiths. (21) (but this probably reflects the projected demographic proportions of the adherents of Muslim and non-Muslim faiths)

Dr.Tan Chee Khoon has pointed out that in Indonesia and Egypt, where the Muslim population is a larger proportion of the whole than in Malaysia, churches and mosques exist side by side, whereas in Malaysia Christians are refused permission to construct churches in land adjacent to mosques. (22) Paul Ing and Theresa Ee refer to how heads of Christian schools were instructed to remove crucifixes from class rooms. (23) The motivations for these prohibitions could be two-fold. One, that the proximity of non-Muslim structures and symbols might pollute Muslim sacred space and might compromise the intense monotheism of Islam (as opposed to what Muslims view as the diluted monotheism of the Christian Trinity). Secondly the churches and non-Muslim icons might in some way attract Muslims or divert their attention from their own faith. Preservation of their commitment to the Islamic faith seems to be a priority for the Malay/Muslim community and the UMNO administration. A third reason is also alleged that Muslim sensibilities might be offended by the public display of these objects. Professor Mohammed Abdul Rauf takes very seriously the outdoor display of things (Hindu and Buddhist idols, perhaps crucifixes) opposed to Muslim *tawhid* (oneness of God) as a provocative offence against Muslim conscience. (24) It is significant that he considers such a display of icons as as offensive if not more than immodest female dress, consumption of liquor and gambling houses. (25) The prohibition of the Chinese Lion Dance in public is also relevant to the issue of the offensive against non-Muslim symbolic artefacts. In 1982 there was a controversy regarding the definition and intended promotion of the national culture. The administration insisted that Islam was one of the essential elements of the national culture in spite of the fact that almost half of the population is non-Muslim. The DAP, the Chinese-led opposition party protested that the proposed national cultural policy only projected Malay/Muslim culture as the national one, ignoring other cultures which were present in strength in the nation. Mr. Lim Kit Siang pointed out that the present government policy was against the original concept of a multi-racial Malaysia. (26)

Canon Batumalai in his "Inter-Religious Dialogue in Malaysia" discusses the issue of inter- religious dialogue in Malaysia. There are many organisations which are active in this aspect of inter-religious relations such as MIRO, ALIRAN, MCCBHS and INSAF.(27) Canon Batumalai points out that Muslims have not shown much interest in inter-religious dialogue in Malaysia and exhorts Christians and others to try and discern the reasons for the Muslim hesitation in participating in the dialogue process. (28) He advocates also other means of Christians relating to their Muslim compatriots to be discussed later in this chapter.

I have already mentioned the enlightened stand of Christian theological institutions in imparting information about Islam to their trainees, ordinands and other students. Dr. Batumalai, himself a keen student of Islam, mentions that he regularly takes his students of the Seminari Theologii Malaysia to the National Mosque, Kuala Lumpur for a direct experience of Islam and particularly Islamic worship. (29) He also invites prominent Muslim leaders, such as Anwar Ibrahim and Fadulah Wilmot to address his students at the seminary. Canon Batumalai states that the visit of Christians to the Pusat Islam (a section of the Prime Minister's Religious Affairs Department) has resulted in reciprocatory moves by their staff to visit the Christian seminary. (30) Such contacts and initiatives are undoubtedly helpful in developing amicable relationships between the two faiths. I was happy to see that the Sarawak Anglican Theological College that I visited, the House of the Epiphany, taught Islam to the ordinands being trained there.

However, Batumalai mentions moves by fundamentalist organisations that would hinder dialogue and good Christian-Muslim relations. In mid 1987 it seems that the PAS Youth Central committee set up an anti-Christianization Action Committee. A gathering (to oppose Christianization) was organised in Sitiawan, Perak on 29th October 1987 where a leader claimed that 10,000 Malays had been converted to Christianity, (31) a claim which sounds entirely dubious in view of the legal restrictions against proselytising Muslims and the reluctance of the Christian church to engage in evangelisation among Muslims.

A positive factor for good Christian-Muslim relations in Sarawak is the fact that extremist Muslim organisations such as Dar al Arqam has not made much headway in the state. There is just one commune and a school established by the organisation near Kuching. Recently the Federal Government has outlawed the organisation owing to its avowed intentions of overthrowing the Mahathir administration and taking over the country *a l'a* Khomeini, from what they perceive as an un-Islamic administration. Their leader Ashaari Mohammed, who is a mystic as well as fundamentalist politician, is said to have met the Prophet in a dream and learnt of the world's impending end. Ashaari accused Mahathir and the Malaysian government of not doing enough to prepare the Malaysian Muslims for this event. (32) Ashaari is known also to have Messianic aspirations from a long time back (he says he is the Mahdi) and for the Islamicisation of not only Malaysia but the whole of Asia.

The PAS has also not established itself on a sound footing in Sarawak, its membership being confined to just a few students returning from studies abroad, where apparently they have more chances of falling under the influence of fundamentalists from the peninsula than in Kuching. It is also significant that the Sarawak administration has powers to stop the immigration of undesirable individuals hailing from the peninsula as from overseas, and has on occasion used these powers to block the entry of *persona non grata* to the state. It is significant that these powers have been used not only against Islamic fundamentalists but also against foreign Christian missionaries. Since 1992 no foreign Christian missionaries have been working in Sarawak.

The absence of extremist Islamic parties and the fact that BINA the main dawah organisation is liberal and moderate in its perspective of other faiths ensure that Christian- Muslim relations may probably never erupt into the overt and physically violent situation which in Malaysia as a whole with the discriminatory attitudes and policies of the federal and state administrations there is potential for.

One of the matters that Colonel Dunstan pointed out in my interview with him was that the Christians of Sarawak have never united politically. The Muslims of Sarawak, the Malay/Melanau group who lead the ruling BN alliance are quite well organised in the Parti Bhumiputera, and therefore the Islamic sector of the population has gained a position of strength in the body politic, though numerically they are not in the majority. The Christians, though demographically the larger group are divided along ethnic lines, the Dayaks, the Chinese etc. and thus are not able to command a position of strength which as the largest religious group they could have achieved. In a way it is salutary that a nation is not divided politically along religious lines since such politicisation of religion is often not conducive to religious harmony. The experience in India with the BJP (Hindu dominated), the Muslim League etc. prove this.

However in the context of the Muslims uniting politically and attaining a dominant position in political affairs it may become imperative for the Christians also to do so. Otherwise they are liable to lose out, being discriminated against on the basis of religious identity by parties such as the UMNO and Parti Bhumiputera for whom increasingly the Islamic factor is overtaking the ethnic in determining the party identity and ideology.

It is a fact that Col. Dunstan was not actually thinking of the Christians coming together and forming a political party. He was only suggesting that "Christian ministers and members of parliament come together and chalk out ways of improving their community and obtaining assistance from the government to this end." He drew attention to the fact that the Muslims are well organized and their organizations such as BINA ask for and receive support from the government. Colonel Dunstan is of the view that the government is willing to give assistance to the Christians also. "They have no reservations about that", he stated.

As part of the administration himself and a Christian, Colonel Dunstan is naturally optimistic about the government's impartiality. It is true, as we have seen earlier, the pronouncements of Taib Mohammed and other Muslim ministers indicate that though they have a preference for Muslims, and belonging to that community would like to support the Muslims as best they could, they are not totally unfair to other religious communities. Speaking in June 1982, the Chief minister assured the other minority groups that they would get their fair share of the socio-economic progress in the state. [33] [Perhaps the Christians in spite of their numerical superiority (28.5% according to the 1980 census as opposed to Muslims 26.3%) is being looked upon as one of the minority groups of the state]. Tun Abang Openg on December 7th 1988 stated that the Sarawak government will strive for the development and progress of the entire *Rakyat* (proletariat) regardless of their racial origins or religious beliefs. [34] Minister for infrastructure development Dr. Wong Soon Kai, speaking at the 90th annual celebrations of the Sarawak Chinese Methodist Church at Sibu, opined that the people of the state should be grateful for the religious tolerance practiced by the state government. [35] However the experience of Christians, as I have pointed out earlier, is one of frustration at the numerous ways in which their aspirations, whether in employment as in the case of Charles, or in the matter of construction of churches, religious education and other religious matters, have been hindered by Government officials who are non-cooperative and even hostile to them. It is evident that if the state administration is impartial and tolerant such attitudes and policies have not trickled down to the lower echelons. The evident support of the government in both the national and state levels for the Malay/Muslim and the fact that the religious dimension of the Malay/Muslim, which is the favoured group in the nation, is supplanting gradually the ethnic dimension seems to be sending down the wrong signals to the Malay/Muslim dominated bureaucracy and even to the Malay/Muslim population as a whole.

As I have explained in the previous chapter, among the non-Muslim faiths of Malaysia, Christianity is the most committed to proselytization, though the Islamic resurgence and the special favours to Islam by the administration has caused an awakening among the Hindu, Buddhist and faiths other than Christianity. The Muslim attitude to Christianity could partly be explained by the fact that both are keen proselytizing faiths and mission to other faiths is ingrained in their ideology. Theoretically conversion is not possible in Hinduism. All Hindus are believed to be born into a particular caste depending on their actions (*karma*) in a previous life. Buddhists would look upon their religion as a way of life, adherence to the noble eighth-fold path rather than as a set of doctrines or rituals. We have seen that Islam and Christianity have been the main contenders for conversion among the tribal people of Malaysia. As stated earlier the Christians are not very active in peninsular Malaysia in evangelization, but they do engage in missionary work among the indigenous population, Chinese and other non-Muslim populations in Sarawak. This makes Islam and Christianity the main rivals in the proselytizing field in the state.

The manner in which Christianity arrived in Malaysia is also significant. The Portuguese, who were the first evangelising influence in Malaysia were noted for their ruthless methods of conquest, both in the secular and the religious sectors of their activity. They are said to have come bearing the cross in one hand and the sword in the other, an extension of the Crusade in the Iberian peninsula. Armed with Papal bulls authorising them to conquer lands and convert the "heathens" they set about their business in a determined and singularly brutal manner. The impact of the Portugese in the early days of their settlement in Malaysia and other parts of Peninsular Malaysia as on the Western coast of India was highly traumatic and contributed to the social alienation between the Christians and Muslims. The Jesuits, and Francis Xavier particularly, who came later had a better image. Of course Christianity came to Sarawak much later (In the 19th century) and through British missionaries, both Protestant and Catholic, rather than the Portugese. Their *modus operandi of* mission was quite different from that of the early Portugese, and they initiated evangelization through agencies such as schools and hospitals which served the community rather than traumatized them. However, the attitude of the foreign missionaries to other faiths was far from respectful or tolerant. Many were categorised as evil, the very work of the Devil. Most missionaries had little authentic understanding of even major faiths such as Islam and Hinduism. Their approach to other religions was far from being conducive to harmonious inter- religious relations.

The approach of Christian missions to other religions has undergone considerable change in recent times. I have already mentioned the teaching of Islam in most theological training of priests and missionaries of the Malaysian church. No missionary worker goes out nowadays to the field of his activities without gaining a thorough understanding of his prospective proselytes. There is also a sincere desire among the churches in Malaysia for dialogue rather than polemics with other faiths. However the memories of the past linger on, and there are still over-zealous Christians whose attitudes to other faiths echo the medieval times when Islam was looked upon as virtually the work of the Devil and Mohammed as the Anti- Christ prophesied in the Book of Revelation. Paul Chee Ing and Theresa Ee make mention of some Christian groups in the peninsula who made use of films and slides which were derisory of Hinduism in missionary work and provoked resentment among the Hindus. (36) Fortunately there are very few Christians nowadays who hold on to such views and attitudes. Evangelization is no doubt a legitimate activity but respect for other faiths and sensitivity to their feelings is an essential quality for a missionary. It is certain that evangelical zeal and such attitudes are not mutually exclusive. The Bapa Malaysia, Tunku Abdul Rahman, was a keen missionary and the founder of PERKIM. However he always exhorted tolerance, peaceful co-existence and respect for other faiths. He did not advocate the Islamic state in Malaysia, and the universal application of the *Shariah*, and he envisaged Malaysia as a secular nation in the sense of being committed to fundamental liberties for all citizens irrespective of their religion.

Canon Batumalai in his writings suggest many measures for promoting good Christian-Muslim relations. One of the issues he deals with is the question of loyalty to the nation. (37) We often observe the tendency on the part of the majority section of a population to doubt the loyalty to the nation of minority groups. This is partly due to the identifying of the nation with the majority group, that is the characteristics of national identity are defined with reference to the majority group. In an earlier chapter I mentioned how some Hindu leaders of India view the Hindus as the only true citizens of India and Muslims and Christians as adherents of alien religions and therefore alien to the nation itself. A similar perspective seems to be held by many Malay/Muslims regarding Christians and other ethno-religious groups. This feeling is strengthened by the special privileges that the Malay/Muslims enjoy which they feel as underwriting their conviction that they are the true sons of the soil, the original inhabitants of Malaysia. Abdul Latif Bakker, University lecturer, states,

> The coming of immigrants from a non-Malay world has never been at the invitation of the Malays, but was the result of British efforts. The Malays preferred Indonesian immigrants who shared the same language and Islam. (38)

The same sentiment is expressed unequivocally by Mohammed Noor Nawawi of the ABIM. Speaking in March 1986 at a seminar on national culture held in Selangor he stated that "Whether we like it or not, it is an accepted fact the Malays came here first and they have a say in formulating the national culture". (39)

The three formative principles of national culture enunciated by the government are Bahasa Malaysia, Islam and Malay culture, a declaration that should be quite irksome to non-Malay/Muslims in so religiously, ethnically and culturally pluralistic a nation as Malaysia. However the issue of national culture has been made one of the sensitive issues, discussion of which would attract penalties under the Sensitive Issues Act. It is also true that a perspective of national culture based on these principles would be influential in formulating the Malay/Muslim concept of national identity which would make only the Malay/ Muslims true citizens of Malaysia and the others aliens in their own country. Moreover, if the national identity is based on Malay ethnicity and adherence to Islam, the loyalty of the non-Muslims would become highly suspect in the eyes of the majority/dominant community. Speaking from my Indian experience I have often heard the view expressed by many of my Hindu friends that the Muslims of India are not loyal citizens of the nation. According to them, they are more loyal to Pakistan than to India. I have already referred to the statement by Devi Lal, former Deputy Prime Minister of India and the agitation it caused among Indian Christians. [40] It is evident that many Hindus hold the loyalty of Muslims doubtful, considering their affinity to be more to Muslim nations than to India. It is possible that a similar attitude exists among the Malay/Muslims of Malaysia with respect to the non-Malay/ Muslim citizens.

Canon Batumalai puts forward some useful suggestions for action on the part of Christians to actualise and demonstrate their loyalty to Malaysia [41]:

1. Love for the nation: to love Malaysia and its pluralistic society and to accept that the Malays need special help (i.e. accept the N.E.P).

2. Adopt a Malaysian identity, instead of an Indian/Chinese etc. identity. Make greater use of the Bahasa in worship, according to the dictum *"Cintaila Bahasa kita"* (we love our language) and cultivate a more Malaysian image.

3. Participate in nation building. He reminds that the contribution of missionaries and Christian churches to education and medical services is already recognised.

Before loyalty to the nation can be expressed and entrenched in these ways the issue of national identity/culture etc. has to be clearly identified and solved. In a multi-lingual, multi-religious and multi-cultural nation such as Malaysia what do Christians accept as the characteristics of national identity and national culture? Is it to be that of the majority Malay/Muslim, which is not yet an absolute majority? Is it to be a fusion of the Malay/Chinese/Indian/Dayak etc.? It will be difficult for Christians to be loyal to the nation if Islam is to be considered the sole religious principle of national identity. Categorising these issues as sensitive and stifling discussion on these vital matters is not helpful and will not ensure the loyalty of all. The present principles of the formulation of national identity/culture will only ensure the loyalty of the Malay/Muslim, and tend to alienate the others. The memorandum submitted by the Indian association to the government warns that in view of the holistic nature of Islam a national culture based on Islam will have no room for other cultures. (42) They state clearly that the formation of a national culture based on the Malay/Muslim equation would not be acceptable to them. (43) The memorandum by the Chinese also state that

> Whilst stressing the importance of Islam and the Malay culture, these principles deny the significant role that should be played by the cultures and religions of the non-Malays. (44)

Prime Minister Dr. Mahathir evidently considers the characteristics of national identity/culture to be drawn from the majority community and are to be defined by them. He warns the minorities

> loyalty to the nation is a very important criterion for Malaysian citizenship. The dissenting minority if they are true citizens must accept what the majority wills or tolerates. (p 45)

It may be helpful to remember in this context that one of the frequent and often reiterated contentions of communalistic parties in India such as the RSS (who assassinated Gandhi), the Janasangh and the B.J.P. is that only Hindus are the true and loyal citizens of India. They equate national identity with *Hindutva* (Hinduness). This is very similar to the pronouncements of the Malaysian administration regarding national culture--that it should be based on the Malay/Muslim principle. The history of the RSS etc. is one strewn with communal conflict and hostility to the religious minorities, culminating in incidents like the recent destruction of the Babri mosque in Ayodhya and widespread Hindu-Muslim conflict in Northern India. The modus vivendi reached in Sarawak over about two centuries of co-existence by the Muslim and the Christian can only be maintained if the administration is fair and just to all. The present unofficial but de facto discrimination against Christian employees and the restrictions placed on their religious activities, be it in the use of books or religious terms, or on public meetings and broadcasts and construction of churches, need to cease in the interest of good Christian-Muslim relations. Inter- religious dialogue has to be initiated from both sides and conflict in the area of religious proselytisation avoided. The absence of extremist organisations in Sarawak, the moderateness of BINA and its liberal perspective on modernisation etc. are factors conducive to good Christian-Muslim relations. If it is a fact that both communities do not seek to proselytise each other it is a positive factor to this end. However, substantial measures on the part of the government in the sectors of training and employment, and an even-handed approach to the matter of religious education in schools with less interference in the running of Christian schools, and in the maintenance of a Christian ethos in such schools, are needed to ensure that harmonious relations are maintained and enhanced in the future. It is beneficial that Christians are keeping a low profile politically and are not seeking to form a political party on the basis of their faith. Over-politicisation of religion is one of the key factors contributing to religious discord and the over-zealousness of some of the Islamic organisations in Malaysia.

Notes

27. MIRP= Malaysian Inter- Religious Organisation.
ALIRAN= Aliran Kedeseran Negara (National Consciousness Movement).
MCCBHS= Malaysian Consultative Council of Buddhism, Christianity, Hinduism and Sikhism.
INSAF= Inter-faith Spiritual Fellowship.

References

1. Hunt, R., Hing, L.K. and Roxborough T. (1992), *Christianity in Malaysia,* Pelanduk Publications: Petaling Jeya, p. 31.
2. Newton, Brian William (1989), *A New Dawn over Sarawak: the Church and its Mission in Sarawak, East Malaysia,* University Microfilms International: Ann Arbor, pp. 44-45.
3. Saunders, Graham, (1992), *Bishops and Brooks,* Oxford University Press: Oxford, p. 3.
4. Ibid.
5. Newton, op. cit., p. 57.
6. Bruton, Roy (1993), *Farewell to Democracy in Sarawak,* Merlin Books Ltd.: Braunton, Devon, p. 66.
7. Means, Gordon P. (1982), "Malaysia: Islam in a Pluralistic Society, in Calderola C, *Religion and Societies in Asia and the Middle East,* Moulton: pp. 445-496, p. 480.
8. Means, Gordon P. (1992), *Malay Politics, the Second Generation,* Oxford University Press: Singapore, p. 104.
9. Khoon Tan Chee (1984), in MCCBHS, *Contemporary Issues in Malaysian Religions,* Pelanduk Publications: Petaling Jeya, p. 35.
10. Means, Gordon P. op. cit., 1992, p. 104.
11. Chapter 3, p. 41
12. Bruton, op.cit., p.76
13.Means, op.cit. 1982, p.477.
14. Ch. 1, p. 11.
15. Khoon, Tan Chee, in MCCBHS, op.cit, p. 39.
16. Ibid.

17. Ing, Paul Tan Chee, and Teresa, Ee (1984), in Introduction to MCCBHS, op. cit., p. 13.

18. Derauh, Dr. Harun, (Edr) (1992), *Malaysia Year Book 1992-93*, Berita Publishing Sdn Bhd: Kuala Lumpur, p. 27.

19. Yung, Hwa (1984), in MCCBHS, op. cit., p. 91.

20. Ibid., p. 13.

21. Quoted in Soong, Kua Kia (1990), *Malaysian Cultural Policy and Democracy*, The Resource and Research Centre: Kuala Lumpur, p. 44.

22. Khoon Tan Chee in MCCBHS, op. cit., p. 34.

23. Ibid., p. 12.

24. Ibid., p. 57. For an account of the controversy see Soong, op.cit.

25. Ibid., pp. 56-57.

26. Soong, op.cit., p. 18.

28. Batumalai, S. (1990), "Inter- Religious Dialogue in Malysia", *A Malaysian Theology of Muhibbah*, S. Batumalai: Kulal Lumpur, 1990, pp. 124-142, p. 125.

29. Ibid., p. 133.

30, Ibid.

31. Ibid., p. 131.

32. *The Times* dt. 8.8.'94.

33. *Sarawak Gazette*, June 1982, p. 61.

34. *Sarawak Gazette*, December 1989, p. 52.

35. *Sarawak Gazette*, December 1990, p. 67.

36. MCCBHS, op. cit., p. 10.

37. Batumalai, S. (1990), "An Understanding of Christian Loyalty in Malaysia, a Personal Reflection", pp. in Batumalai, S., op. cit., pp. 151-157.

38. Soong, op. cit., p. 16.

39. Ibid., p. 42.

40. In Ch. 4, p. 64.

41. Batumalai, op. cit., p. 155.

42. Soong, Op. cit., p. 258.

43. Ibid.

44. Ibid., p. 214.

45. Quoted in Batumalai, op.cit., p. 124.

6 Conclusion

As Colonel Dunstan remarked Malaysia has a better record of religious harmony than many an other nation. It is a fact that there is no overt persecution of religious minorities nor endemic violent religious conflict, as for instance in the Sudan or Kashmir. However, there is no room for complacency. The existence of fundamentalist organisations, the call for Islamicisation of the state which is to some extent supported by the federal and state governments, the favouritism shown to the Malay/Muslim at the expense of other communities, restrictions in the discussion of religious issues, and authoritarian acts of law such as the Sensitive Issues Act, are factors which have the potential for building up into an explosive situation on the ethno/religious front. The increasing politicisation of religion and the frustration of Christians and other minority religions regarding employment, freedom for proselytisation, restrictions on and hampering of building their places of worship etc. are quite palpable. The bodies formed to promote religious harmony, the National Unity Board, ALIRAN and MCCBHS have not been able to achieve much in the face of governmental policies and restrictive legislation, though their very existence is a cause for hope. The goal of the majority group and the administration is Islamicisation of the state in the long run. While the Islamic state is not a totally unviable proposition and has many commendable features, in such a pluralistic setting as Malaysia or Sarawak that may not be the best way of governing the nation. The universal implementation of an inflexible system of law which is to a great extent incompatible with the modern situation will not be acceptable to what is essentially, excluding the Muslims, almost the majority of the population in Malaysia. Even nations in which Islam is an overwhelming majority have run into difficulties in implementing an Islamic/theocratic state. In matters of the economy such as banking, and penal law, the democratic process, gender issues etc. the institution of the Islamic state has thrown up enormous problems. In a way the association of the state with religion has more merit to it than its being entirely divorced from religious faith. Rev. Hwa Yung points out that morality and ethics without a religious basis will be devoid of reason. (1) He quotes Sartre who is said to have remarked "If I have excluded God, there must be a somebody to invent values". (2) Rev. Yung was talking of moral education in schools, but his point may well be relevant to national life as a whole. But the association of the state with religion, even when it is attached to one particular faith as in Malaysia, should not assume a form which makes it difficult for adherents of other faiths to participate in national life or make them feel left out or discriminated against. Negata opines that in Malaysia, the association that the state had with Islam in earlier days was acceptable to all. (3) But the present Islamic resurgence, and the rivalry between the government and Islamic fundamentalists in the *dawah* activities have retarded the concosiational process and has led to increased religious polarisation. Islam can effectively function as a civil religion in Malaysia if the choice of rituals, symbols etc. are such that they are acceptable to Muslims and non- Muslims alike. It seems to me that an association of this kind with one particular religion in a pluralistic society has necessarily to be symbolic without going into much detail of ritual and doctrine. The Islamicisation of the state is an entirely different matter.

Nevertheless the association of the state with a religion, seems much more preferable to an entirely irreligious and even anti-religious situation as in the former Soviet Union. In India, Gandhi had attempted with some success, to incorporate elements from the major religions of India into public events, a practice which continues there even today on days of national importance such as Independence Day, National Integration day and Martyrs' day (anniversary of the Mahatma's death). The reading of different scriptures, and prayers by leaders of the various religious communities have been usefully incorporated into public ceremonies and national celebrations. Such a public display of religious tolerance and acknowledgement of religious diversity would be quite salutary and helpful for national unity. National celebrations and state ceremonies would then reflect the multi-religious character of the nation rather than stressing the dominance of one particular faith.

In a way Malaysia is fortunate that its Muslim/non-Muslim populations are so well balanced. This demographic balance is a curb on the excesses which are associated with absolute power. It is also a positive factor that the governments of the Federation as well as in Borneo are coalition governments. The give and take, the compromises and adjustments such coalitions entail are beneficial for inter-factional harmony. The UMNO and the Sarawak Parti Bhumiputera ideology is on the whole moderate and aligned to non-discriminatory ideals though these parties are under pressure from more fundamentalist and extremist parties, and prone to appeasing what they apprehend as aspirations popular with the majority Malay/Muslim group, though not entirely in conformity with what their judgement advocates as the best course to take for national unity or harmony. Though Sarawak has not even accepted Islam as the official religion Tun Abang Opung a member of the cabinet stated that Sarawak would be the first of the Malaysian states to implement the *Shariah*. (4)

One of the obstacles to religious and racial concord, is the reluctance of the Malay/Muslim group to admit the highly pluralistic and diverse nature of Malaysian society. Tunku Abdal Rahman recognised this diversity, and though he still demanded a special status for Islam opposed the wholesale implementation of the Islamic state and the *Shariah* on all the people. The present leadership, probably under pressure from competing pro-Islamicisation factions, seem to be increasingly attuned to the idea of the Islamic state at least in the long term and the dominance of the Malay/Muslim group. Judging from their pronouncements regarding national culture they seem to ignore the fact that the Malaysian culture is a composite of Malay/Chinese/Indian/Dayak etc. cultures. The UMNO-led administration and the Malay/Muslim factions would seek to impose this to some extent monolithic culture, based on Islam and Malay culture than anything else, rather than permitting the natural evolution of a composite culture in which all the above mentioned traditions fuse harmoniously. Worse still they do not permit discussion of the issue of national culture, seemingly categorising it as one of the sensitive issues such as the religion of Islam, the Rukunegara and race. Both Mahathir and Anwar Ibrahim as well as other UMNO leaders have warned the Chinese and others against discussing the issue of national culture openly. [5]

In Sarawak the demographic pattern peculiar to the state is not permitted to have its full impact on questions of identity, culture, and public life in general owing to the fact that it is part of the Federation, and the Malay/Melanau faction which leads the administration are protegees of the UMNO and loyal to the UMNO ideology. This is a complete negation of pre-independence trends, the Brookes especially being keen to preserve the special characteristics and indigenous traditions of the region. The status of the Dayaks and the Christians would have been entirely different if the state had not come so much under the control of the UMNO/Parti Bhumiputera ideology and policies. The fact is that in spite of the numerically inferior status of the Malay/Muslim group in the island, the situation is only marginally different from that of the Peninsula. The Malay/Melanau leadership accuse the Dayak-led PBDS of racism. Chief Minister Taib Mohammed warned that the state will be thrown into chaos if the government yielded to pressure from one race. (6) The minister for infrastructure assured the Dayaks and other groups that their future had nothing to do with the Chief Minister's race (The Chief Minister belongs to the Melanau tribe). (7) Chief Minister Taib reiterated that the Barisan Nasional government with its multi-racial composition is the best for the country. (8) The state government is portrayed as multi-racial and anti-racist, and the PBDS as racist, by the Malay/Melanau Muslim caucus. However in spite of the coalitionary nature of the state administration--what is termed "consociational democracy"--there is a danger that the Malay/Melanau faction in the coalition has tended to dominate at the expense of the other partners, leading to their hegemony in the political and administrative field. A scrutiny of the PBDS manifesto for the 1991 state elections seems to indicate that the PBDS is as committed to race equality and justice for all ethnic groups as anyone else (Please see appendices 2 and 3). The Malay/Melanau group is held together by Islam and therefore the fact that the state administration is led by this group gives an edge to Islam in all matters. The fact that a large section of the Dayaks are Christians imparts much significance to the BN/PBDS confrontation for Christian-Muslim relations. The 1991 election victory for the BN was only marginal. It remains to be seen whether a PBDS victory in the future will ameliorate the present discriminatory, restrictive and frustrating experience which the Christians of Sarawak allege. The Dayaks and the Chinese form the major Christian constituency in Sarawak and it is significant that during the referendum for the question of cession with the Federation only one third of the Dayaks agreed to the merger of Sarawak with Malaysia and the vast majority of the Chinese opposed it.(9) The larger proportion of Malays favoured cession.(10) It is a fact that merger with the Federation has been advantageous to the Malay/Melanau Muslim group.

The Malay/Muslim equation and the special status it has acquired along with economic promotion seem to be very significant factors in the growing polarisation of Malaysian society both ethnically and religiously. This identity of race and religion is particularly significant for Christian-Muslim relations and in Sarawak assumes greater importance because of the fact that demographically the Christians are the biggest religious group there, whereas politically they are marginalised in comparison with the powerful Malay/Melanau Muslim group. However the fact that many of the Christians hailing from the Ibans and other indigenous groups are also eligible for special privileges as Bhumiputra should mute to some extent the frustration. But, in reality, as we have seen in the case of Charles and other Christians, in spite of the Bhumiputra status they are still victims of discrimination in favour of the Malay/Muslim . The fact is that the ruling UMNO and Parti Bhumiputera are in favour of Malay/Muslim ascendancy and even the Islamicisation of the state in the long term, though as Chandra Muzzafar remarks they have a different means of achieving it from the ultra-radical Islamic groups. [11] There is a possibility that as the religious element of the Malay/Muslim equation becomes dominant the Islamic factor will cut across ethnic lines and may eventually supplant the Malay identity altogether. The Father of the Nation Tunku Abdal Rahman had always argued for the absorption of all Muslims into the Malay identity. If this happens the Malay/Muslim may attain a clear numerical majority as contrasted with its present nominal majority and the circumstances of the Christians and other non-Muslims become even more marginalised in the nation. While in the Peninsula Christians are a very small proportion of the population and the impact of the Islamicisation of Malay/Muslim identity will not alter very much the situation in inter- religious terms, it may considerably exacerbate Christian-Muslim relations in Sarawak with its scenario of a substantial Christian population. One would tend to agree with Jayum Jawan that the prognosis for stability in Sarawak is not very good. [12] Besides, the trend under Dr. Mahathir is towards an increasingly strong Federal government and the restriction and even suppression of dissent. Sarawak would undoubtedly be affected by the increasingly Islamicising ideology of Dr. Mahathir, Anwar Ibrahim and the UMNO/ Parti Bhumiputera. Unless the policies and attitudes of the federal and state leaders, especially those who head the coalition governments at the Centre and Sarawak, alter radically, the situation is bound to create increased tension between the Muslims and others in Malaysia, and in Sarawak especially between the Muslims and the largest non-Muslim religious community, the Christians. Increasing tensions within these coalitions are inevitable if the UMNO/Parti Bhumiputera do not take into consideration the non- Malay/non-Muslim grievances. The absence of legislation against discrimination such as the Race Relations Act of Britain is quite striking. It will be salutary that instead of categorising the three R's of Race, Religion and Rukunegara as sensitive issues and stifling discussion, the government would adopt an enlightened policy of enacting legislation against discrimination on the grounds of ethnicity/religion. However there may be temptation in the present background of Islamic resurgence to go down the slippery slope of further bias for and support of one ethnic group/religion at the expense of others.

The administration and the Malaysian leadership could endeavour to rise above "party political" considerations and envisage a policy of according special economic/employment/educational opportunities to all races and religious groups on the basis of individual economic status. Nothing could promote national unity and harmonious inter-ethnic/inter- religious relations than such a policy. It would obviate much of the frustration experienced now by poor Chinese/Indian/Christian citizens who can find no way forward for bettering their circumstances. As I have mentioned in the introduction the NEP does not seem to have profited even all the Malay/Muslims. [13] Certainly privileges and special rights based on economic status seem to be much more fair and just than a blanket regulation of special rights for one community, however politically expedient it may be.

Islamic revival is a global phenomenon and it is not strange that a nation such as Malaysia which has a substantial Muslim Population should be part of the revival process in the Islamic Umma. I have in an earlier chapter tried to briefly unravel the underlying reasons for Islamic resurgence. (14) As a nation newly freed from a colonial power and seeking a new identity, and flexing its new found muscles after independence, Malaysia has caught onto Islam as one of the ways of asserting this new identity. The symbols of Islam such as grandiose mosques, Islamic turbans and *hijabs*, Qur'an reading competitions etc. are important in this resurgence, but as Haji Tawfeek pointed out are not the vital and essential aspects of Islamic revival. The more aggressive forms of fundamentalism are fortunately rare in Malaysia, though Muslim extremists did at one time desecrate some Hindu temples. (15) In 1984, one of the more extremist proponents of fundamentalism, Ibrahim Libya, led a confrontation in Memali with the police in which several people were killed. Dar- al - Arqam has recently been banned due to its increasing militancy and its avowed intention of overthrowing the government. It is fortunate that in Sarawak *dawah* activities are mainly confined to BINA, a moderate organisation.

However it is sad that Islamic revival in Malaysia as in other parts of the Muslim world is so backward looking. This negates the inherent dynamism of Islam, as though it does not have the potential for adapting to the needs and circumstances of the modern world. The proponents of Islamic revival seem to be harking back to the conditions of a time which however glorious cannot be relevant to the changed situation of the world today. Islamic law was not wholly formulated by the Prophet, though the Qur'an and the Ahadith constitute its main basis. Its development was through the deliberations of later ulama (scholars) who employed *idjma, qiyas* and other methods for deriving the legal regulations. Moreover Schacht has pointed out that it has absorbed much from other legal systems of the day such as Jewish law and Roman law and also from local traditions and pre- Islamic practice of the great centres of Islam--Damascus, Basra, Mecca, Kufa et-al. (16) The process of *idjma*(consensus) of the Ulama, one of the *usul* (roots) of the *Shariah* is said to have been adapted from the Roman concept of *opinio prudentium*. But why such adaptability should be denied Islamic law in modern times is perplexing. Unfortunately the position of the orthodoxy, is that no modification of the Islamic law is possible after the 10th century A. D. The gates of *ijtihad* (personal interpretation of scriptures) is said to be closed now. The Islamic University of Malaysia and the champions of Islamic revival have to think about and devise new ways of making Islamic law relevant to the needs of modern times, rather than harping on rigourous adherence to what was evidently formulated for a context and situation which no longer exists.

It would have been much better if revival had been based on a model such as that set by Sayyid Ahmed Khan. Sir Sayyid was responsible for the revival of the Islamic community of India, dejected and lapsing into greater and greater backwardness after its traumatic experience at the hands of the British in the wake of the rebellion of 1857. Rejecting Western education and modernisation, the Muslim community of India had very little involvement or say in the administration of the country, and was being rapidly overtaken by the Hindu and Christian sections of the population. Sayyid Ahmad Khan's radical and innovative Qur'anic hermeneutics gave a new ideological impetus to the Muslim community of India, leading to its ascendancy in the latter period of the British era and eventually to the creation of Pakistan. Sir Sayyid argued that there was no inherent contradiction between Islam and Science. His new interpretation of the scriptures sought to remove superstition and backwardness from Islamic ideology and scriptural exegesis. His Islamic revival was essentially dynamic and progressive and not backward looking. He championed the use of *Ijtihad* and while he promoted the Wahabi ideology and the Arabic/Urdu language he advocated simultaneously the adoption of useful elements of Western culture such as disciplined habits, etiquette, more efficient use of time, as well as scientific learning and technological expertise. He avidly promoted good Muslim-Christian relations pointing to the close historical and doctrinal roots of the two faiths and the highly exalted status of Jesus in the Qur'an. He advocated the study of each other's scriptures. In this way he was a pioneer of Muslim-Christian dialogue in India and at the same time a champion of Islamic revival. (17) The Sayyid Ahmed model of revival would have certainly been advantageous to improving inter-religious relations in Malaysia, and the prosperity of the nation in general.

Malaysian Islamic organisations such as the PAS and the ABIM are said to be profoundly influenced by the happenings in Iran. The fundamentalists seem to be following the ideology of Ayatolla Khomeini in their concept of Islamic revival and the islamicisation of the state. Perhaps Ali Shariati was more influential on the Iranian people than the Ayatollah, though unfortunately he was assassinated before the overthrow of the Pahlavi regime, presumably by the Shah's secret service, the SAVAK. Shariati's concept of the Islamic state was highly egalitarian, the *tawhid* of unity as he stated supplanting the *shirk* of a society divided by class, race and wealth. Ali Shariati envisaged religion as an ennobling and stimulating power raising human existence to the highest realms of experience, rather than the stultifying factor which according to him it had become, keeping human experience at a dull, animal- like level and restricting human freedom. He characterised the Prophet as having brought the greatest revolution in human history. (18) This is perhaps what the Islamic resurgence in Malaysia should aspire to do--raise the values, and quality of life, be progressive and attuned to the needs of the modern world, promote harmony with other faiths and generally be dynamic and forward looking in building up the nation.

It seems that for good inter-religious relations and in general for national integration the Christians of Malaysia need to shed the rather Western image which they now project and try make their community truly indigenous. As Canon Batumalai remarks" Christians cannot remain a 'potted plant', alien to the Malaysian soil in their religious practices and even lifestyle. (19) The indigenisation and contexualisation has already begun. The Christians have to adopt elements from Malaysian culture in church architecture, rituals, music and the language of worship. These need not compromise the essential beliefs of the Christian faith. The European missionaries brought a Christianity which was clothed in Western cultural garb. But Christianity originated in Asia, not in Europe, and more important still it is an universal religion. Imitating Sadhu Sundar Singh's famous statement, the Christians of Malaysia should be able to serve "the Water of Life in a Malaysian cup". The government and the Malay/Muslim population on their part have to abandon their reservations against Christian usage of the Bahasa and Islamic religious terms. But how will you define Malaysian culture? The national culture is not solely determined by the Malay/Muslim language, religion and customs. The Christians have to look beyond this to the Chinese/Indian/Dayak cultures also for the indigenisation process.

Christian-Muslim relations in Sarawak has not deteriorated and may perhaps never will to open conflict. But there is much frustration, misgivings and hidden anger in the Christians at being denied their rightful place in society; and at the bias for the Malay/Muslim and Islamic revival on the part of the administration. They question this 'most favoured community' status for the Malay/Muslim, at least in Sarawak, where numerically Christians are stronger though not organised politically. This frustration, shared by the non-Malay/Melanau section in general, seething underneath, has the potential for exploding into open conflict, though their discontent is at the moment suppressed by restrictive regulations, such as the ISA and the Sensitive Issues Act. The *Rukunegara* (National Ideology) is a very positive and viable document. The administration in co-operation with the MCCBHS and ALIRAN and other such conciliatory organisations should work to implement the Rukunegara in letter and spirit and foster better inter-ethnic/religious harmony.

Malaysia in general and Sarawak in particular has rich resources, a colourful culture and intelligent and able peoples. It has therefore great potential for advancement. The state of Christian-

Muslim relations is a significant issue in this province with its substantial populations of both communities. Good Christian-Muslim rapport and cooperation can raise the region to heights of prosperity rarely achieved in the third world.

Notes

17. For an account of Sir Sayyid's life and work see Malik, Hafeez (1980), *Sir Sayyid Ahmad Khan and Muslim Modernization in India and Pakistan*, Columbia University Press: New York.

18. For an account of Ali Shariati's Concept of the Islamic State see Algar, Hamid (1983), *The Roots of the Islamic Revolution*, The Open Press: London, pp. 78-82.

References

1. Yung, Hwa (1984), in MCCBHS, *Contemporary Issues in Malaysian Religions*, Pelanduk Publications: Petaling Jeya, pp. 85-91, p. 91.
2. Ibid.
3. Negata, Judith (1984), *The Reflowering of Malaysian Islam*, University of British Columbia Press: Vancouver, p. 240.
4. *Sarawak Gazette*, July 1991, p. 44.
5. Soong, Kua Kia (1990), *Malaysian Cultural Policy and Democracy*, The Research and Resource Centre: Kulala Lumpur, pp. 17 and 31.
6. *Sarawak Gazette*, September 1990, p. 47.
7. *Sarawak Gazette*, July 1991, p. 47.
8. *Sarawak Gazette*, April 1991, p. 62.
9. Jayum, Jawan (1991), *The Ethnic Factor in Modern Politics: The Case of Sarawak, East Malaysia*, University Centre for South East Asian Studies, University of Hull: Hull, p. 70.

10. Ibid.

11. Muzzafar, Chandra (1982), *Islamic Resurgence in Malaysia*, Penerbit Fajar Bakti Sdn Bhd: Petaling Jeya, p. 33.

12. Jayum, op. cit., p. 10.

13. Ch. 1, p. 12.

14. Ch. 4, pp. 51-55.

15. See Schact, Joseph (1964), *An Introduction to Islamic Law*, Oxford, Clarendon Press: Oxford, pp. 19-22.

16. Ibid., p. 20.

19. Batumalai, S.(1990), "An Understanding of Christian Loyalty in Malaysia, A Personal Reflection", in Batumalai, S., *A Malaysian Theology of Muhibbah,* S. Batumalai: Kulala Lumpur, pp. 151-157, p. 154.

Table 1
Sarawak
Religion and population
percentage of total population

	1947		1960		1970		1980	
	No	%	No	%	No	%	No	%
Christian	43,069	7.9	117,755	15.8	171,335	17.6	370,500	28.5
Muslim	134,318	24.6	174,123	23.4	229,590	26.3	341,900	26.3
Buddhist					76,334	7.8	213,200	16.4
No religion	368,998	67.5	452,651	60.8	147,191	15.1	153,400	11.8
Other					262,842	26.9	182,000	17.0

Table 2
Sarawak
Distribution of religious groups by ethnicity (1970)

	Malay	Melanu	Iban	Bidayuh	Chinese	Others
Muslim	177,374	38,155	648	170	465	12,778
Christian	209	4,152	51,774	39,203	45,329	30,668
Buddhist	12	14	244	187	75,664	213
No Religion	369	5,150	69,046	7,823	61,753	3,050
Other	244	4,822	152,177	35,930	56,358	13,334

Table 3
Sarawak
Population and its distribution
by ethnicity

Ethnicity	Numbers (000)			Percentage		
	1960	1970	1988	1960	1970	1988
Iban	238	303	471	32	31	30
Bidayuh	58	84	133	8	8	8
Orang Ulu	38	51	86	5	5	5
Malay	129	181	330	17	19	21
Melanau	45	53	92	6	6	6
Chinese	229	294	463	31	30	29
Others	8	10	18	1	1	1
Total	745	976	1593	100	100	100

Bibliography

Books

Abdullah, Firdaus Haji (1985), *Radical Malay Politics, Its Origins and Early Development*, Pelanduk Publications: Singapore.
Algar, Hamid (1983), *The Roots of the Islamic Revolution*, The Open Press: London.
Ali, S. Hussain (1981), *The Malays, Their Problems and Future*, Heinemann Asia: Kuala Lumpur.
Angkatan Nahadathul Islam Bersatu (United Islamic Renaissance Movement) (1993), *BINA, A Brief Introduction*, BINA: Kuching.
Antoun and Hegland (Edrs.) (1987), *Religious Resurgence*, Syracuse University Press: New York.
Arbee, Ahamad Rejal,(Edr) (1992), *Malaysia Information*, Berita Publishing: Kuala Lumpur.
Batumalai, S.(1990), *A Malaysian Theology of Muhibbah*, S.Batumalai: Kuala Lumpur.
Brundage, J. A., *The Crusades, Motives and Achievements*, D. C. Heath and Co.: Lexington.
Bruton, Roy (1993), *Farewell to Democracy in Sarawak*, Merlin Books: Braunton, Devon.

Chin, S.C., Devaraj, J., Jin, C.K. (1989), *Logging against the Natives of Sarawak,*, Insan (Institute of Social Analysis): Petaling Jeya.

Ching, Yu Loon (1987), *Sarawak, The Plot that Failed*, Summer Times Publishing: Singapore.

Endicott, K.M., (1970), *An Analysis of Malay Magic*, Oxford University Press: Singapore.

Enloe, Cynthia H.(1970), *Multi-ethnic Politics, The Case of Malaysia*, Center for South East Asian Studies, Research Monograph No.2, University of California: Berkeley.

Fan Yew Teng (1989), *The UMNO Drama: Power Struggles in Malaysia*, Egret Pubns: Kuala Lumpur.

Funston (1980), *Malay Politics in Malaysia*, (UMNO & PAS), Heinemann Asia: Petaling Jeya.

Gabrielli, Francesco (1969)*Arab Historians of the Crusades*, (Costello, E. J, Tr.), Routledge and Kegan Paul: London.

Geertz, C. (1971), *Islam Observed*, University of Chicago Press: Chicago.

Geertz, C. (1960), *The Religion of Java*, University of Chicago Press: Chicago.

Glick, T.F. (1979), *Islamic and Christian Spain in the Early Middle Ages*, Princeton University Press: Princeton.

Hick, J. (Edr), (1977), *The Myth of God Incarnate* , SCM Press: London

Hunt, R., Hing, L.K., Roxborough, J., (Edrs) 1992),   *Christianity in Malaysia*, Pelanduk Publications: Petaling Jeya.

Hussin, Muttalib (1990), *Islam and Ethnicity in Malay Politics*, Oxford University Press: Singapore.

Islamic Council of Europe (1979), *Concept of Islamic State*, Islamic Council of Europe: London.

Jawan, Jayum, A (1991), *The ethnic Factcr in Modern Politics, The Case of Sarawak, East Malaysia*, University of Hull Centre for South East Asian Studies: Hull.

Kroeber, A.L. (1967), *Anthropology*, Oxford and I.B.H., Publishing Co.: New Delhi.

Jusoh, Hamid (1991), *The Position of Islamic Law in the Malaysian Constitution*, Dewan Pustaka dan Bahasa Kementerian Pendidikan Malaysia: Kuala Lumpur.

Kasimin, Amran (1991), *Religion and Social Change among the Indigenous People of the Malay Peninsula*, Dewan Bahasa dan Pustaka:

Kuala Lumpur.

Khoon, Tan Chee (1985), *Malaysia Today*, Pelanduk Pubns: Petaling Jeya.

Kris, Jitab (1991), *Sarawak Awakens, Taib Mohammed's Politics*, Pelanduk Pubns: Petaling Jeya.

Kumar, G.Siva (1991), *Taib, A Vision for Sarawak*, Jakaman Sdn Bhd: Kuching.

Legal Research Board (1993), *Malaysia Education Act, 1965*, International Law Book service: Kuala Lumpur.

MCCBHS (1984), *Contemporary Issues in Malaysian Religions*, Pelanduk Publications: Petaling Jeya.

Means, Gordon, P. (1992), *Malaysian Politics, The Second Generation*, Oxford University Press: Singapore.

Means, Gordon P.(1982), " Malaysia, Islam in a Pluralistic Society" in Caldarola, C., *Religion and Societies in Asia and the Middle East*, Moulton, pp. 445-496.

Merad, Ali (1981), "The Ideologisation of Islam in the Contemporary World", in Cudsi, A.S., and Dessouki, A.E.H., *Islam and Power*, Croom Helm: London, pp. 37-48.

Mohammed, Mahathir (1986), *The Challenge*, Pelanduk Publications: Petaling Jeya.

Muzzafar Chandra, (1987), *Islamic Resurgence in Malaysia*, Penerbit Fajar Bakti Sdn Bhd: Petaling Jeya.

Negata, Judith (1984), *The Relflowering of Malaysian Islam*, University of British Columbia Press: Vancouver.

Newton, B.W. (1989), *A New Dawn over Sarawak, The Church and its Mission in Sarawak*, University Microfilms International: Ann Arbor.

Osman, Mohammed Taib (1985), *Malaysian world View*, Institute of SE Asian Studies: Singapore.

Rahman, Tunku Abdul (1984), *Contemporary Issues in Malay Politics*, Pelanduk Pubns: Petaling Jeya.

Ratnam K.J. (1965),*Communalism and the Political Process in Malaya*, University of Malaya Press: Kuala Lumpur.

Reece, R.H.W. (1982), *The Name of Brooke, The End of White Rajah Rule in Sarawak*, Oxford University Press: Kuala Lumpur.

Regan, Daniel (1977), "Secular city, The Religious Orientation of Intelllectuals in Malaysia", in Lent, John A. (Edr), *Cultural Pluralism in Malaysian Polity, Military, Mass Media, Education Religion and Social*

Class, North Illinois University Centre for South East Asian Studies: Illinois, pp. 43-56.

Ritchie, James (1993), *A Political Saga, Sarawak 1981-1993*, Summer Times Publishing: Singapore.

Roff, William R. (1967), *The Origins of Malay Nationalism*, Yale Univ Press: New Haven.

Rogers, Marvin L. (1993), *Local Politics in Rural Malaysia*, S S Majeed & Co. Publishing division: Kuala Lumpur.

Runciman, S. (1964), "The Crusades, a Moral Failure", in Brundage, J. A., *The Crusades, Motives and Achievements*, D. C. Heath and Co.: Lexington, pp. 75-81.

Schact, Joseph (1964), *An Introduction to Islamic Law*, Clarendon Press: Oxford.

Sheikh, M. S., (1982), *Islamic Philosophy*, The Octagon Press: London.

Soong, Kua Kia (1990), *Malaysian Cultural Policy and Democracy*, The Resource and Research Centre: Selangor.

Saunders, Graham (1992) *Bishops and Brookes*, Oxford University Press: Oxford.

State Attorney General's Chambers, Kuching (1981), *The Constitution of Sarawak*, Govt Printers: Kuching.

Suffian Tun Mohamed (1988), *An Introduction to the Legal System of Malaysia*, Penerbit Bakti Sdn. Bhd: Petaling Jeya.

Yegar, Moshe (1979), *Islam and Islamic Insttiutions in British Malaya*, The Magna Press: Jerusalem.

Journal Articles

Bakar, Mohammed Abdu (1981), "Islamic Revivalism and the Political Process in Malaysia", *Asian Survey* 21, No. 10, October, 1040-59.

Daniel, J.R. (1990), "Cultural Life Of Indian Christians In Peninsular Malaysia", *Sarjana*, Jilid 6, June, pp. 37-51.

Drahman, A.N.A. (1993), " Historical Development of Education in Sarawak", *Sarawak Gazette*, December, pp. 14-19.

Fawcett, F. (1897), "The Moplahs of Malabar", *The Imperial and Asiatic Quarterly Review*, October, pp. 288-299.

Jawan, Jayum A. (1993), "The Sarawak State General Election of

1991", *Kajian Malaysia*, vol XI, No 1, June, pp. 1-22.

Kessler, Clive S.(1980), "Malaysian Islamic Revivalism and Political Dissatisfaction in a Divided Society", *S.E.Asian Chronicle*, October, pp. 3 -11.

Langub, Jayl (1993), "Native Adat or Customary Laws of Sarawak: an Overview", *Sarawak Gazette*, June, pp.5-9.

Lee, Raymond, L.M. (1990), "Secularisation and Religious Change in Malaysia as a Testing Ground", *Sarjana*, June, pp. 69-81.

Mauzy, Diane K., and Milne, R. S. (1983-84), "The Mahathir Administration in Malaysia, Discipline Through Islam", *Pacific Affairs*, 56, no.4, (Winter), pp.617- 648.

Sundaram, J.K. and Ahamed, Shabarey Cheek (1988), "The Politics of Malaysian Islamic Resurgence", *Third World Quarterly*, 10, No.2, April, pp.843-868.

Troll, C.W., (1979) "Christian-Muslim Relations in India", *Islamo Christiana*, No. 5, pp. 119 to 145.

Various issues of *Sarawak Gazette* and *Sunday Tribune*.

The Times, London, 8th August 1994.

Appendix 1
Political parties of Sarawak

Barisan Nasional (BN)

The Barisan Nasional (National Front) is a grand coalition of various communal parties; its main components in the Peninsula are the UMNO, MCA and the MIC. In Sarawak, the Melanau-led multi-indigenous PBB, the Chinese-dominated multi-ethnic SUPP, and the Chinese-led, Iban-dominated SNAP comprise the present state-level BN (or more specifically BN3); however, the PBDS is a component member at the federal-level. Since its formation in 1976, the state-level BN has been led by the PBB (i.e. the PBB president is also Chairman of the Sarawak BN); at the federal level, it has been led by UMNO.

Barisan Nasional Plus (BN Plus)

Barisan Nasional Plus was a temporary electoral arrangement introduced by Taib Mahmud in 1983; specifically it refers to the Sarawak state level BN, comprising the PBB, SNAP and SUPP, plus the newly formed PBDS. After the 1983 election, the Barisan National Supreme Council admitted PBDS as a full member at the state and federal levels.

Barisan Nasional Tiga (BN Tiga or BN3)

Barisan Nasional Tiga (BN3) is a coalition of three political parties (i.e. the PBB, SUPP and SNAPP) after the withdrawal of PBDS from the state level Barisan Nasional in 1987. But, the PBDS is still a component at the federal (national) level.

Barisan Rakyat Jati Sarawak (BARJASA)

Barisan Rakyat Jati Sarawak, the second Malay party, was formed in 1961. The formation of (BARJASA) reflected divisions within the Malay community; (BARJASA) was anti-cessionist favouring the status quo of Sarawak as the British Crown Colony, while PANAS was in favour of Sarawak's independence from Britain. Among the prominent leaders of the party were Tunku Bujang, its founder President, Taib Mahmud, Rahman Yakub and Abang Han Abang Ahmad. In 1967, it merged with the other Muslim party, PANAS, to form Parti Bumiputera, the backbone of the Alliance governments formed after the 1970 and 1974 state general elections.

113

Malaysian Chinese Association MCA

Since independence, the Peninsula-based MCA has been the main political party representing (Peninsular) Chinese interest in the state and federal governments. However, its popular support from the Chinese Community has varied. Its main rival is the Peninsula-based Democratic Action Party (DAP).

Malaysian Indian Congress (MIC)

Since independence, the peninsula-based MIC has been the main political party representing the Indian interests in the federal and state governments.

Parti Bansa Dayak Sarawak (PBDS)

Parti Bansa Dayak Sarawak was formed in July 1983 by former Iban leaders of SNAP who were dissatisfied with the leadership of James Wong. Among the more prominent of these leaders were Datuk Leo Moggie, Datuk Daniel Tajeim and Joseph Mamat Samuel who became the founder President, Deputy President and Secretary-General respectively. In 1987, it withdrew from the State-level BN, but maintained its membership at the federal level.

Parti Bersatu Sabah (PBS)

Parti Bersatu Sabah is a Kadazan-dominated multi-ethnic party. It was formed in March 1985 amid rising discontent among the peoples of Sabah for the excessive behaviour of the ruling Parti Berjaya (BERJAYA). PBS ousted BERJAYA in 1985 by winning slightly more than 50% of the seats in the state assembly. Due to the general instability of the party's position arising from several events aimed at toppling it, PBS went into another election in 1986; this time, the party won two-thirds of the state seats. In 1990, it was again returned to power. However, despite its general popularity, the party's rule has been turbulent because it does not enjoy the favour of the federal UMNO leaders. During the parliamentary election of 1991, the party withdrew from the BN and aligned itself with Semangat 46, a splinter party of some Malay leaders opposed to the Peninsula based UMNO.

Parti Bumiputera (BUMIPUTERA)

Parti Bumiputera was formed in 1967 from the merger of the Melanau-dominated BERJASA and the Malay-dominated PANAS. The prominent leaders of BERJASA, Rahman Yakub and Taib Mahmud, went on to dominate the leadership of the newly-founded BUMIPUTERA. See also BERJASA and PANAS

Parti Negara Sarawak (PANAS)

Parti Negara Sarawak was formed on 9 April 1960. The party grew partly out of the perceived need to unite the Sarawak natives in order to protect them against the growing influence of the SUPP, and partly as a response to the anti-cession movement ; PANAS was in favour of Sarawak's independence from Britain. Although a multi-ethnic party, it was dominated by the Malay Abangs (aristocrats): Abang Mustapha was its founder President, while his brother, Abang Othman, was the Secretary-General. In 1967, it merged with BARJASA to form Parti Bumiputera.

Parti Pesaka Anak Sarawak (PESAKA)

The Parti Pesaka Anak Sarawak was formed in 1962 to unite the Rejang Ibans; they were not adequately represented in SNAP. It was led by *Temenggong* Jugah, who was then PANAS Vice-president; he had to be persuaded to leave PANAS and lead the party as its founder President. PESAKA was one of the component parties in the first state Alliance party system; it provided the candidate for the Chief Ministership after the removal of Kalong Ningkan in 1966. In 1973, it merged with BUMIPUTERA to form the Parti Pesaka Bumiputera Bersatu (PBB)

Parti Pesaka Bumiputera Bersatu (PBB)

The Parti Pesaka Bumiputera Bersatu was founded on January 1973 on the merger of PESAKA and BUMIPUTERA. *Temenggong* Jugah, the Federal Minister for Sarawak affairs and the President of PESAKA, was elected as its founder President, while Taib Mahmud and Rahman Yakub were elected its founder Vice-President and Secretary-General respectively. Since the merger, the Malay/Melanau wing has dominated the party.

Sarawak Alliance

The Sarawak Alliance, the state component of the National Alliance, emerged from the transformation of the Sarawak United Front and consisted initially of SNAP, PESAKA, BARJASA, PANAS and SCA. Until the Alliance party system was restyled Barisan Nasional in 1976, it had provided Sarawak with its first three Chief Ministers: Kalong Ningkan (SNAP), *Penghulu* Tawi Sli (PESAKA) and Rahman Yakub (BUMIPUTERA).

Sarawak Chinese Association (SCA)

The Sarawak Chinese Association was formed in 1962 as a result of the perceived need for an alternative party for the Chinese who would not support the SUPP. As the SUPP was seen as too left-wing it was felt that a moderate alternative acceptable to the government could represent the Chinese in the coalition government. With the formation of the Alliance, SCA had been the Chinese representative in government, although it received considerably less Chinese Support in Sarawak than the SUPP. It was dissolved in 1974 and most of its members joined SUPP.

Sarawak National Party (SNAP)

The Sarawak National Party established on 10 April 1961 was the first Iban party formed by the Saribas or Second Division Ibans. It was also associated with the new Iban leaders, who were characteristically different from the PESAKA's traditional (community) leaders--they were educated. Of the founder members, Stephen Kalong Ningkan, who was its first Secretary-General, was the best known, having been the first Chief Minister to be unconstitutionally removed. In 1983, its power base was eroded when many second generation Iban leaders left the party, when a Chinese, James Wong, took over its leadership.

Sarawak United People's Party

The Sarawak United People's Party, which was formed on 12 June 1959, is the oldest political party in Sarawak. SUPP grew out of the need to centralise the many Chinese social and commercial organisations in order to better protect their interests. Although a multi-ethnic party, the native Iban and Malay members have never exercised any real power. Since 1970, when it forged a coalition with BUMIPUTERA(later PBB), SUPP has been the source of strength of the PBB-led coalition.

United Malays National Organisation (UMNO)

Since independence in 1957, the majority of the peninsular Malays have supported UMNO, with the exception of pockets of Malays in the east coast states of Kelantan and Terengganu, who have backed the religious-based Parti Islam Se-Malaysia (PAS), which presently controls the state government of Kelantan. Until the mid-1980s, PAS was UMNO's main rival for Malay support, but lately there has been an UMNO splinter group which formed Semangat 1946 (S-46), and, in the 1991 elections, led nation-wide opposition to the UMNO-led Barisan Nasional. But the PAS-64-led opposition managed to secure only the state of Kelantan, and many of its members are now slowly rejoining UMNO. Since independence, UMNO has been the pillar of the coalition government (state and federal--with the exception of the present leadership in the states of Kelantan and Sabah).

United Sabah National Organisation (USNO)

A Sabah-based party dominated by Muslim Sabahans, it is presently the main opposition party in the state; at the federal level, it is a component of the Barisan Nasional. The current status of the party is uncertain. With the recent entry of UMNO into Sabah, most of its elected federal and state representatives have pledged support for UMNO Sabah and in fact, its president, Tun Mustapha, has joined UMNO.

Appendix 2
Barisan Nasional Sarawak Manifesto 1991

BN Sarawak Government pledges a better future for all

Preamble

Under the State Barisan Nasional Sarawak Government led by YAB Datuk Patinggi Tan Sri Haji Abdul Taib Mahmud, Sarawak has experienced tremendous progress. The State economy grew rapidly at an average rate of 6.6% per annum, and the per capita income grew from $2,745 in 1981 to $3947 in 1990 in real terms. This rapid growth of the State economy was achieved despite the severe recession of the mid 1980s.

At the same time, we have started to restructure our economy so that the State becomes less dependant on the export of timber, crude petroleum and a few primary commodities. As a result, the contribution of the manufacturing sector to the Gross Domestic Product has increased from 6.6% in 1981 to 14.5% in 1990. Similarly, tourism has been developed to play a greater role in our efforts to widen the base of our economy. No doubt with this success the

Government will intensify its efforts to bring about a further strengthening of the State economy for sustained growth and prosperity.

Impressive progress has also been made in the social fields, especially in education and health services. These services no longer benefit only the well-to-do group in the urban areas. They are now readily available to most households including those in the most remote rural areas. The number of school children, both in primary and secondary levels, has increased from 310,000 in 1981 to 360,000 in 1990 which practically represents the entire school-going population in Sarawak. At the same time, more opportunities are now available to our youths to pursue tertiary and technical education within the State with the establishment of the UPM Campus in Bintulu, ITM and IKM Campuses and a Polytechnic in Kuching. We are now working towards the eventual development of UPM as a full-fledged university in Sarawak. Similarly, medical and health services are now within easy reach of the people. During the last decade, the number of rural health centres and clinics, for example, has increased from 211 in 1981 to 271 in 1990 - an increase of more than 30%.

During the same period, not only have we achieved progress in education and health, but significant improvement has also been made in the provision of basic amenities throughout the State. In 1981, for instance, only 35% of all households in the State had electricity supplied to their homes. The Barisan Nasional Sarawak Government, through its rural electrification programme, has succeeded in increasing this proportion to 64% by 1990. Similarly, the percentage of households supplied with treated water has almost doubled during the last 10 years: that is, from 32% in 1981 to 61% in 1990. In the rural areas, too, the percentage of houses supplied with treated water has increased from 20% in 1981 to 47% in 1990.

The above improvement--i.e. increase in income, expansion of educational and health services, improved provisions of basic amenities, etc., has contributed to a drastic drop in the incidence of poverty in the State from 31.8% in 1984 to 21% in 1990 and from 37% in 1984 to 25% in 1990 in the rural areas.

Amidst all this achievement, the Barisan Nasional Sarawak Government has not forgotten the importance of preserving and promoting our rich traditions and cultures which are now the pride and joy of Sarawakians and the envy of its visitors.

Our Barisan Nasional Sarawak has strengthened the foundations for a progressive and prosperous society wherein everyone lives in peace and harmony, We must now build upon these foundations a better future for all as envisaged by our Wawasan 2020.

1. Peace, Stability and Progress Through Politics of Development

   BN Sarawak brings peace, stability and progress for the people of Sarawak through Politics of Development.

2. A More Caring Society

   The BN Sarawak Government is committed towards developing a more caring society: the less privileged and less fortunate members of our society will continue to receive our special attention.

3. Proper Management Of Our Natural Resources

   The BN Sarawak Government guarantees the proper and efficient management of our natural resources which will be sustained for our future generations.

4. Greater Opportunities For All

   BN Sarawak Government translates the State's development potentials into opportunities for all the people of Sarawak, both in the urban and rural areas.

5. Human Resource Development

   BN Sarawak emphasises education and training in its human resource development to meet the present and future needs of our State, particularly in the technical and scientific fields.

6. Preservation of Our Rich Cultural Heritage

   BN Sarawak preserves and promotes the rich cultural heritage of our peoples and maintain our tradition of making Sarawak a confluence of our varied cultures.

7. Upholding BN Sarawak Spirit of Cooperation

    BN Sarawak Government ensures close cooperation and active participation of all communities in the administration of the State and maintains a close working relationship with the Federal Government.

8. Increased Pace Of Economic Development

    BN Sarawak Government will continue to intensify its efforts to achieve a rapid and sustainable growth of the State economy for the benefit of all by providing more infrastructural facilities, expanding industries and opening up more land for development as well as accelerating the process of land settlement.

Let us continue to achieve more development for a better future

Appendix 3
Parti Bansa Dayak Sarawak Manifesto

Change for a fair and better future

Parti Bansa Dayak Sarawak upholds the Rukun Negara,

The Malaysian System of Parliamentary Democracy wherein each community plays a meaningful part;
AND as the Government in the State of Sarawak, believes in and will uphold the rights and privileges of all communities fairly, justly and judiciously with the provisions as enshrined both in the State and Federal Constitutions.

And to this end Parti Bansa Dayak Sarawak

AFFIRMS that the Yang Di Pertuan Agong is the custodian of the rights and privileges of all communities;
AFFIRMS that the languages and culture of the various communities be accorded appropriate status while recognising Bahasa Malaysia as the National Language;
BELIEVES in the freedom of worship while accepting Islam as the official religion of the Nation;
BELIEVES in the concept of meaningful power sharing in spirit, form content and policy;
BELIEVES in benevolent implementation of social economic and political development;
BELIEVES in maintaining, peace security and harmonious relationship amongst all communities;
BELIEVES in the individual right to property, and that no person shall be deprived of his property without adequate compensation;
BELIEVES in upholding the rule of law, the supremacy of the Constitution of Malaysia and of the State of Sarawak and that no one shall be unjustly discriminated against by reason of his race or creed;

The present Government has failed

*   in nurturing racial harmony;
*   in eradicating the politics of fear and nepotism;
*   in distributing Sarawak's wealth equitably but instead enriching only the few;
*   in reducing the incidents of poverty among some communities; in providing employment opportunities to school leavers;
*   in nurturing high morale in the civil service and statutory bodies;
*   in providing adequate complementary assistance to the federal educational programmes for deserving and needy students;

* in solving land ownership problems;
* in providing land to the genuinely landless citizens;
* in implementing many agricultural and development programmes;
* in carrying out balanced development between urban and rural areas;
* in the proper stewardship of the State natural resources;
* in giving assistance to the National Registration Department to issue Birth Certificates and Identity Cards to all Sarawakians who still do not possess them;

Change all these now

And accepting the responsibility to take immediate steps to correct these failures PARTI BANSA DAYAK SARAWAK pledges the following:

1   Democracy and multi-racialism

Recognising Malaysia as a multi-racial society where peace and prosperity depend on racial harmony, we pledge:

* to eradicate the politics of fear and nepotism that has been practised in Sarawak, and to ensure a fair and just society where every race can enjoy their rights, privileges and opportunities;
* to make Sarawak a place and a home for everyone of its citizens;
* to ensure the practice of parliamentary democracy in which elections must be held fairly and freely and that no citizen shall be penalised for exercising their democratic rights;

2   Economy

Whereas the present Government fails to distribute wealth and opportunities equally to everyone in the State, we pledge:

* to ensure an equitable and fair distribution of the opportunities for economic development irrespective of race, creed or politics;
* to encourage local participation in economic and business opportunities;
* to review and redefine the roles of public corporations in line with the privatisation policy of the Federal Government so as not to compete with the existing business interests in the State;
* to urge the Federal Government to declare Sarawak as a Special Development Zone.

3   Employment

Whereas the present State Government has failed to provide employment opportunities to the mounting number of school leavers, we pledge to ensure greater employment through:

* creating more skill-training programmes to correct the mismatch between employment requirements and labour force supplies;
* embarking upon urbanisation programmes for rural areas;
* locating resource-based industries, including timber, within or near concession areas;
* implementing various programmes which will encourage the employment of local people.

4   Civil service and statutory bodies

The Civil Service machinery and Statutory Bodies play a key role in providing services and in implementing the State development programmes. Unfortunately, the Civil Servants and employees of Statutory Bodies have been subjected to unnecessary political pressures in their duties which have affected their morale and performance. We pledge:

* to ensure that the Civil Service and the management of Statutory Bodies remain impartial, professional, clean and efficient;

* to ensure that recruitment , promotion, in-service training , and opportunities for career development within the Civil Service and Statutory Bodies be fair to all;
* to ensure that the management of the State Statutory Bodies reflects the racial composition in the State;
* to ensure that officers in the Civil Service and Statutory Bodies will not be forced to participate in partisan politics.

5   Education

Recognising that a substantial percentage of the population of Sarawak are unable to acquire the necessary level of quality education. We pledge:

* to ensure that every child gets the basic level of education;
* to urge the Federal Government to re-examine and to implement programmes to improve the quality of education given to the rural students.
* to provide complementary programmes to give more facilities to rural students;
* to increase educational assistance to deserving needy students in the forms of scholarships and loans including the setting up of revolving fund for this purpose;
* to provide annual grant of not less than 5 million dollars to all independent Chinese and Mission Schools and Government aided Chinese and Mission Primary Schools;
* to continue to urge the Federal Government to site a full-fledged University in Sarawak.

6   Land policy

Whereas the present land policies and administration fail to address land ownership. We pledge;

* to formulate land policies which will ensure a more equitable land ownership, especially for those who are in genuine need of land;
* to ensure that the rights of the Native Customary Land owners are honoured and protected;

* to expedite the survey of the Native Customary Land in the State with the aim of providing individual titles to the land owners;
* to formulate policies that would enable the alienation of State Land to the landless for farming and housing;
* to ensure that all private land frozen under Government Compulsory Acquisition Orders pursuant to section 47 of the Land Code (Sarawak) and other similar provisions in the Ordinance of Statutory Bodies for over 2 years and not used for any public purpose be lifted forthwith;
* to review the existing land legislation in order to safe-guard the legitimate interests of the landowners;

7 Agriculture and land development

A proper agriculture and land development plan is important for the economy of Sarawak. The present agriculture and land development policies and implementation fail to achieve the expected results because of the insensitivity to local needs and traditions. We pledge:

* to open more State Land for the establishment of private plantations;
* to thoroughly consult landowners where land development involves private land, including Native Customary Right Land, to ensure that the landowners can effectively participate in, contribute towards and benefit from such development:
* to modernise smallholding agriculture by intensifying in-situ development programmes and by upgrading the existing agriculture support services such as subsidy schemes, training and extension;
* to draw practical programmes to increase the income of farmers;
* to review the administration of Land Development Agencies in order to improve their efficiency and to ensure that they are accountable to the rakyat;
* to formulate long-term agriculture strategies for the State to meet the challenges in the next 30 years.

8   Urban and rural development

There is unbalanced development between urban and rural areas in the present time. We will change this. We pledge:

*   To make it our priority to provide the rural as well as urban population with basic amenities like:
    -clean running water and electricity
    -roads and bridges
    -medical facilities
    -better housing
*   to extend credit facilities, meaningful assistance, and proper marketing system for farmers and fishermen;
*   to continue to allocate adequate funds to ensure the growth of urban areas;

9   Natural resources

The natural resources of the State belong to all citizens and not in the hands of a privileged few. The income from them must be fully utilised to develop Sarawak for the benefit of all.

Timber

We pledge:

*   to ensure that the forests of Sarawak be exploited on a sustainable yield basis so that our future generation will continue to benefit from it;
*   to take immediate steps to reduce the export of logs and ensure that the concession owners set up timber-related down-stream industries;
*   to award timber concession on the basis of an Open Tender System and that the concession will be awarded after a thorough Environmental Impact Assessment(EIA) Study has been carried out;
*   to review the Forest Ordinance, and if necessary to amend any of its provisions and pass further legislation to ensure mutual benefits of the people and the State;
*   to safeguard the legitimate interests and business investments of timber companies so that they continue to make contributions toward the social-economic well being of the people and toward the development of the State;

*   to ensure that the rural dwellers benefit from logging activities in their areas;

Mining

We pledge

*   to give fair equity participation to those whose livelihood are directly affected by mining activities;
*   to make social amenities for the local populace be part of the package deal for mining an area;
*   to give people in the affected area priority over jobs except in the case of specialised work where local expertise is not available.

Petroleum

We pledge to make proper representation to the Federal Government on the following:

*   to encourage joint-venture companies with local participation for the exploration and exploitation of the State's oil and gas deposits;
*   to give local contractors ample opportunities to participate in contract and sub-contract works in the exploration of oil and gas resources;
*   to ask the company awarded the contract to explore and extract oil and gas to draw up a training Programme for local personnel as part of its involvement towards the localisation of manpower needs;
*   to give bigger development allocation to Sarawak for the development of the State infrastructures since oil and gas, which are produced substantially in Sarawak continue to become a major source of revenue for the Nation.

10   Industrial development

The development of industry will be one of the main economic activities in the future. In our recognition of this, we pledge:

*   to draw up industrial master plan for the State;

*   to ensure that the processing of application to set up industry in the State be done expeditiously through the setting up of a one-step agency;
*   to identify and encourage the development of new industrial sites to meet the new industry in the future;
*   to promote small and medium size industries to match the technological, financial and resources availability in the State;
*   to assist in the creation of labour-utilising domestic and cottage industries in the rural areas;
*   to encourage more new foreign and domestic investments in the State;
*   to monitor the undesirable side effects of the tourist trade and industry while we promote and encourage its development in the State.

11   Poverty eradication

The incidence of poverty among some communities in the State has increased. There is no serious efforts by the present Government to reduce the incidence of poverty among these communities. We believe in a caring society.

We pledge:

*   to give top priority towards the relief and development programmes of poverty eradication;
*   to form a Task Force to identify poor households in the State and to ensure that these groups receive proper assistance so as to improve their economic status.

12   Birth certificates and identity cards

A mounting number of people born and bred in the State do not possess Birth Certificates and Identity Cards. All of them have experienced repeated difficulties in obtaining these documents.

We pledge:

*   to assist the National Registration Department to organise a State-Wide National Registration Exercise with the aim of

issuing Birth Certificates and Identity Cards to every legitimate Sarawakians in the State;

* to provide, if necessary, State funds and manpower to assist the National Registration Department in this exercise;
* to assist the National Registration Department to locate owners of Birth Certificates and Identity Cards which are still with the department;
* to assist the National Registration Department to ensure that no person acquires Malaysia Residential Status and Citizenship through unlawful means.

13   Matters of special interest

There are matters which appear small and unimportant to the present State Government, but nevertheless, are important to the people of Sarawak. To this end, we pledge:

* to review the existing policies on shot guns with the aim of permitting the purchase and replacement of shot guns by genuine farmers;
* to return or compensate for the shot guns that are now being retained by the Government during the emergency to their owners;
* to examine the possibility of giving a dollar for dollar grant for the building of religious institutions in the State.

14   State-federal relations

We re-affirm that Sarawak is an inseparable part of Malaysia. We believe that a close relationship between the State and Federal Government is vital for national unity and integration. Towards this end, we pledge:

* to ensure that our Government will always be a member of the Federal Barisan Nasional Government;
* to discuss matters of State and Federal concern amicably and sensibly as members of the same family;
* to work for closer rapport between the State and Federal leadership.

Conclusion

Sarawak is a State with a multi-racial populace endowed with rich natural resources. These natural resources are the heritage of all Malaysians in Sarawak. They must be developed for the benefits of all citizens and not be monopolised by the privileged few.

Do not allow the inequalities that are rampant among us to continue

You can change all these....he power to change is in your hands. Vote for a change. Vote for PBDS. Avote for PBDS is a vote for a fair and better future for you.